Affinity Publisher
for
Ad Creatives

AFFINITY PUBLISHER FOR
SELF-PUBLISHING - BOOK 2

M.L. HUMPHREY

SELECT TITLES BY M.L. HUMPHREY

CONTENTS

INTRODUCTION

In *Affinity Publisher for Fiction Layouts* I walked readers through how to use Affinity Publisher to create a print layout for a novel, short story collection, or other work of fiction.

Eventually I will also do the same for non-fiction books which require a few additional skills such as the ability to insert images within the text of the document, the creation of tables of contents and an index, as well as combining multiple Affinity files into one book. Those books both share a common approach to Affinity Publisher and are in line with the main expected use of the program.

But because I'm cheap and lazy, I also use Affinity Publisher for the creation of basic book covers as well as my ad creatives for things like Amazon A+ Content and Facebook ads.

In reality, the ideal product for covers is probably Affinity Photo not Publisher because it's the program you'd use for things like photo manipulation, but I'm not a skilled graphic designer so I don't do that with my covers.

For ads, though, Affinity Publisher is a great choice since you're mostly combining existing elements into a new image and that can definitely be done with Publisher.

So that's what we're going to focus on in this book: how to use Affinity Publisher to create ad images.

The examples in this book are going to be for Amazon A+ content, Facebook ads, and BookBub CPC ads, but you can easily apply what we're going to do here to any website graphics. Basically, if you know the dimensions you're working with for an online image, you should be able to create it when you're done with this book.

Specifically, we will cover how to:

- Create a cover image for use in Amazon A+ Content Comparison Chart listings

- Create a combined image with all of your series covers for use in Amazon A+ Content

- Create a square Facebook ad that uses your book cover for the background

- Create a square Facebook ad that uses an image for half of the ad

- Create a BookBub CPC ad image with various image adjustments and a 99 cent label

We will walk through from start to finish how to do each of the above. This means that at times we will repeat certain skills. While each project will be presented on a standalone basis, I'd recommend that you work through the projects in order because we'll be building up your skills as we progress through the book. The first time I present a skill I'll do so in detail, but the next time I present it I'll do so in a much shorter manner.

For example, it's very easy to create the cover image to use in Amazon's A+ Content. Very easy. But that also requires a handful of basic skills that we can cover in a very low-pressure setting before we use them on other projects that are more complex.

Also, once you've gone through the book you can reference the Appendix at the back for a quick refresh on each of the skills we covered if you happen to forget the details of how to do it. That will save having to read through a lot of pages just to find out how to do X.

Now, keep in mind I am not a graphic designer. Nor am I a cover design or advertising professional.

I am a self-taught self-published author who learned these skills because I have little to no patience to wait for others to do things for me. If my Facebook (FB) ad isn't working, I want to change out that image today not three weeks from now when my designer can fit me in and at a cost of $25. (If I'm lucky to have someone that responsive and cheap that I can reach out to.)

What we're going to do here should be accessible to any user willing to put in the time and effort (and maybe do a little math, but not much), but don't expect to be some sort of high-level design guru when we're done. If there are special secrets out there, I don't know them.

I will also add that I absolutely believe every self-published author should master the basics of what we're going to cover here. Because the profit generally is not there as you're building up your audience to pay for slick marketing materials that a professional created. And, honestly, they're not needed for 99.9% of authors. Especially if you have a strong cover and use that in your ads. Because the cover is going to be doing most of the heavy lifting for you in terms of catching your audience's attention.

Also, mastering design basics will help you better judge the quality and appropriateness of any design work you do pay for, whether that's for your cover, your website, or your ads. Hopefully this book will also help you understand how easy or difficult something is to do. (For example, the first cover I ever paid for was an unmanipulated stock image that almost anyone could've put together in ten minutes, but I didn't know that at the time.)

Now, keep in mind when you're starting out with design work that you're probably going to make some mistakes or not have the skills to create the product you want. But just like with writing, you'll get better with practice, so don't give up on it.

As long as you're willing to try, fail, try again, fail again, try again, and succeed, you can get there. And I would bet good money that some of you who read this book will leave me in your dust in terms of where you end up.

The goal of this book is not to present myself as some untouchable expert but to instead share with you the foundational skills that I've learned.

Okay. So with that said, before we dive in on our first project I think it's important that we discuss some basic design principles that will help you create better images.

BASIC DESIGN PRINCIPLES

This is going to be a very high-level review of design principles. Ideally you should read more about it either online or by purchasing any of a number of books that are out there that cover these concepts. The two books on my shelf that are applicable to this are *The Non-Designer's Design Book* by Robin Williams and *Thou Shall Not Use Comic Sans* from Peachpit Press, but I'm sure there are others out there that also cover these concepts and are perhaps even better resources than those two.

I've also found a number of online articles and blogs that touch on these concepts, a few of which I'll mention below. This information is readily available for those who go looking.

Through all of this keep in mind that your goal is to (1) get the attention of *readers* who will like *your* type of book and then to (2) get them to click through and buy or download that book. Every design decision you make should revolve around those considerations.

With that said, let's start with color.

COLOR

There's actually a lot to think about with respect to color so remember that this is just a crash course.

GENRE-SPECIFIC

Most genres or categories use a specific color palette.

Many years ago and under a different pen name I published a few books about online dating. If you go and look at the books for men for online dating you'll see that for many of those books the colors that are used are white, black, red, and bright yellow.

In contrast, the colors that are used for books about online dating for women are white, black, and either pale or bright pink.

(I just double-checked and it looks like orange may be making its way in there as well for men, but even eight years later this still holds.)

This means that the very first thing you need to do before you choose your images or prepare an ad is look at books like yours and see what colors are in use in your genre or category.

This is probably more important when designing covers, but I think it is still important for ads. You can easily lose a reader if you don't use the colors that readers expect.

Say, for example, you're writing paranormal romance. If your colors are white, black, dark green, yellow, and gray that will confuse readers, because those colors don't really signify paranormal romance.

And I will add here that this is why it's good to read your genre because, especially on the Amazon storefront, books get so miscategorized that it can be tricky to do this research properly.

I just looked there to confirm my instinct that paranormal romance is usually a lot of bright purples and blues with some swirly movement involved. But there were books there by authors I wouldn't personally categorize as paranormal romance. Fantasy romance, yes. Paranormal, no.

So be careful and ideally look at authors who you know write what you write.

And if you don't know comparable authors, like I didn't for my romance titles, one place to look if you already have sales is at your also-boughts and also-reads on your book's product page. Although that can be biased by how you originally branded your title and the cover you chose, so it may not be perfect either, but it will at least get you closer to the target.

Also, you should know not only the colors for your genre, but the colors for your sub-genre, too. Romance is a huge genre, for example, and darker romance has a different color palette (dark background with white, red, bright yellow, maybe some lighter purple or turquoise text) than sweet and wholesome romance (white background with white, pink, light yellow, pale blue, lilac).

There are also color trends that can influence this, so make sure your research is current. I'd say color trends are more important on the non-fiction or literary fiction side than the genre fiction side, but they happen across all genres. Like the recent trend for a darker turquoise color on covers, and I believe it was a bright orange before that.

So. Genre and sub-genre appropriate and keep an eye on trends.

MEANING

The next thing to understand about colors, and this may be more for non-fiction than fiction or already baked into the genre-specific colors, is that colors have associated emotions and meanings.

I have a printout from some website called thelogocompany.net from 2013 that is a Color Emotion Guide. Looks like it's still available here: https://thelogocompany.net/psychology-of-color-in-logo-design/

It shows that colors like gray are for peace and calm whereas colors like red are for excitement or boldness. It also shows various brands that use those different colors. So, Fanta, for example is orange because it's a friendly, confident, and cheerful brand.

It's been a while since I did research on the meaning of color, but as I recall, not everyone agrees on the meaning behind every color.

Also, keep in mind that different colors have different meanings in different cultures. So one color may work great for the U.S. market but not for the Chinese market. I primarily sell in the U.S. so that's the market I design for, but if you're marketing say, a German translation, then it would be a good idea to know the meaning of different colors in Germany.

While there is likely no single definitive answer on color meaning you should at least have some idea about whether the ones you've chosen fit the book you're advertising.

A bright yellow color in an ad for a brutal, dark horror is going to attract the wrong reader because yellow is generally a happy, positive color.

(Unless it's clearly done in some sort of ironic way in which case that packaging better be spot on from ad through to book description. Because, again, the goal of ads and covers is to (a) attract someone to purchase your product, but to also (b) make sure it's the right person so they buy more from you later. Everything you do needs to be in alignment to pull in the *right* reader not just any reader. And that includes the colors you choose for your ads and covers.)

Now let's go into some more high-level color choice issues.

COLOR PAIRS

There is a reason so many movie posters use the colors orange and teal, and that's because orange and teal are considered complementary colors, they sit opposite one another on a color wheel.

A color wheel is created by taking the three primary colors, red, blue, and yellow and then combining them to get the secondary colors of purple, green, and orange. And then combining each secondary color with its neighboring primary colors to get tertiary colors such as yellow-orange, yellow-green, etc.

When in doubt about which colors to pair with one another, take the first color you want to use, like teal, and look directly across the color wheel to find the color that is opposite it, in this case, orange.

This is usually going to be an effective pairing.

Another option if you want a more subtle pairing is to stay with the same basic color but change the saturation or the brightness so that you pair a dark blue with a lighter shade of the same blue. This is essentially moving along a line drawn from the center of the color wheel to the outer edge.

(We'll see a color wheel later in Affinity. If you don't want to wait for that they're ubiquitous online, just search for color wheel.)

PRINT VERSUS SCREEN COLORS

Another issue you need to be aware of with respect to color is the difference between print color and screen color.

Ads and covers are designed on a computer screen, but the way that color is created on a computer screen is not the way that color is created when printed.

A screen uses what's called RGB colors which are created by combining different lights. RGB colors are brighter and more saturated and have a wider range of possibilities. Print uses CMYK colors which combine different inks.

For the ads we're going to be creating in this book, it's not going to be a big issue because we'll create on a screen and users will view on a screen. But do keep in mind that different displays will display colors differently. So, for example, I work on a PC but I also have a Mac and when I look at the same file on both computers, there is a clear difference between them. So know that your audience may see the image differently simply because they're viewing it on their hardware instead of yours.

CONTRAST

Another color issue to keep in mind when designing ads is that you want people to be able to see and absorb the key components of your ad.

This is why white on black and black on white are so common in signage because they contrast one another so strongly that you can see the text without struggle.

Some color combinations are horrible for contrast. I have seen the advice given, for example, to never put red on black or black on red. It's simply too hard to see. (I've broken this one before and currently have some covers that break this one, but it is true that it's harder to see.)

Whatever colors you choose, make sure that they contrast one another enough that your chosen elements are clearly visible to your audience.

(I say chosen elements because in some cases maybe we're not talking about text. For a fantasy my strongest ad element could be a dragon image. For a sexy romance ad it could be a hot guy. Whatever the element is that is supposed to draw in your reader, make sure it stands out. This is not the time for subtlety.)

Alright. That was the crash course in color, now on to element placement.

ELEMENT PLACEMENT

Element placement revolves around where you place each element of the design. This can be the book cover, review quote, ad image, promotional information, etc. There are tricks to make the placement of your elements more effective.

RULE OF THIRDS

One of the simplest ways to decide how to place the elements in your project is to use the rule of thirds. Take your document workspace and divide it into three horizontal sections and three vertical sections so that you end up with nine total sections.

If you can, you should then try to place pivotal elements at the intersection of these lines. The strongest intersection is the one in the top left corner.

You can also place the different elements of your design within the sections created by the grid to create a clean separation. Or line up a key portion of your image (such as the horizon or a tree or figure) along one of the lines.

This article by Cover Designs Studio (https://www.coverdesignstudio.com/layout-rule-of-thirds-diagonal-scan-and-more/) has a more detailed discussion of how this works and shows some real-life examples from trade-published book covers.

THE GOLDEN RATIO

Sometimes the rule of thirds can feel a little boring and basic. One of the ways I've experimented with mixing it up is trying to incorporate the golden ratio into my designs instead.

This basically involves using a rectangular space that has sides that are in the ratio of 1 to 1.618. You can then turn that on its side and create another, smaller rectangular space with the same ratio. Keep doing that and you end up with a series of smaller and smaller squares and a spiral down to a central point that will draw the eye.

Place a key element of your design in that central spot and it will be a more effective design.

I've tried using this with FB ads that use multiple images. I'm not sure I've been personally successful in those experiments. But the world abounds with examples of people who have successfully leveraged the golden ratio.

(Another possible way to use it is to use the 1.6 ratio when determining the relative font sizes of different text elements in your design.)

LEGIBILITY

The other key thing to keep in mind when creating an ad image is where and how your audience will view the image. In a FB feed, you don't want subtlety. This is not the time to have the outline of a dark gray dragon overlaid upon an even darker gray background.

If your ad doesn't convey something worth stopping for and clicking on, it's not an effective ad.

Now on to fonts.

FONT

Ah, font. So important and so easy to get wrong. This category covers the text choices you make—the actual font you use as well as its size and arrangement. It's much more important in cover design than in ad design, but we'll touch on a few key points at least.

TYPES AND HISTORY

Certain fonts are associated with key moments in history or have a bad reputation. (See Comic Sans for an example of a bad reputation.)

For example, if you find some cool font that you think will be just perfect for your project, maybe look it up first to make sure you aren't using the same font that was used for Word War II propaganda.

GENRE OR CATEGORY-SPECIFIC

Also, once more we run into the issue that certain genres or categories tend to use certain fonts or at least types of fonts. So, for example, a cursive font that looks like a woman's handwriting is more likely to be used for romance than for a thriller which is probably going to use a sans-serif font with some thickness to it instead.

If you're going to veer away from standard fonts for your ads, keep this in mind. Does the font match the genre or category of the book you're advertising? This is about conveying a consistent tone to your audience that tells them "this is the kind of book you want". If there's conflict between the font you use and the cover image, they probably won't click.

HIERARCHY

The important elements in your ad should be the largest elements in your ad. You don't want your audience's eye drawn to the wrong part of the ad first. Using a larger font size is one way to draw attention to key elements.

LEGIBILITY

Font can convey tone and genre outside of the words that are written, but if you're also trying to highlight a good quote, for example, you'll want your audience to be able to read the text of that quote. Always check that your ad will be legible at the size it will be seen by your audience which is often going to be much smaller than the size you design at.

* * *

Alright. That was your crash course in design elements. It's not everything, but it should be enough to get us started.

And if you want to dive in further on these topics there are many, many resources out there. The internet has any number of websites about design and there are a handful of free courses through Coursera and other sites.

Although I will say that I personally find the ones geared toward graphic design in general a bit annoying. I like to get to the point and those courses sometimes want to show me how to make artistic designs using an apple as a stamp or will spend an hour discussing the history of fonts. Zzzz.

Anyway. We're ready for our first project now, but first I want to talk about how to set up your workspace in Affinity when working with images like ads or covers.

AFFINITY WORKSPACE

I have Affinity Publisher set up very differently when I'm working with covers or ad creatives compared to when I'm laying out a book. By using Studio Presets I can switch back and forth between the two without having to reconfigure my workspace each time.

I already covered this in *Affinity Publisher for Fiction Layouts* from the print layout perspective, so if you've read that book and already created a workspace for images, then you can skim this section. But I expect that there will be enough readers who wanted to learn ad creatives but not book layouts that I better cover it again here to be safe.

(I am going to skip over the "what is Affinity" and how to open it portion, though.)

Okay. So setting up your workspace.

First I'm going to show you my workspace with a simple project already open so you can see the various components you'll be working with as you do your design work.

Here we go:

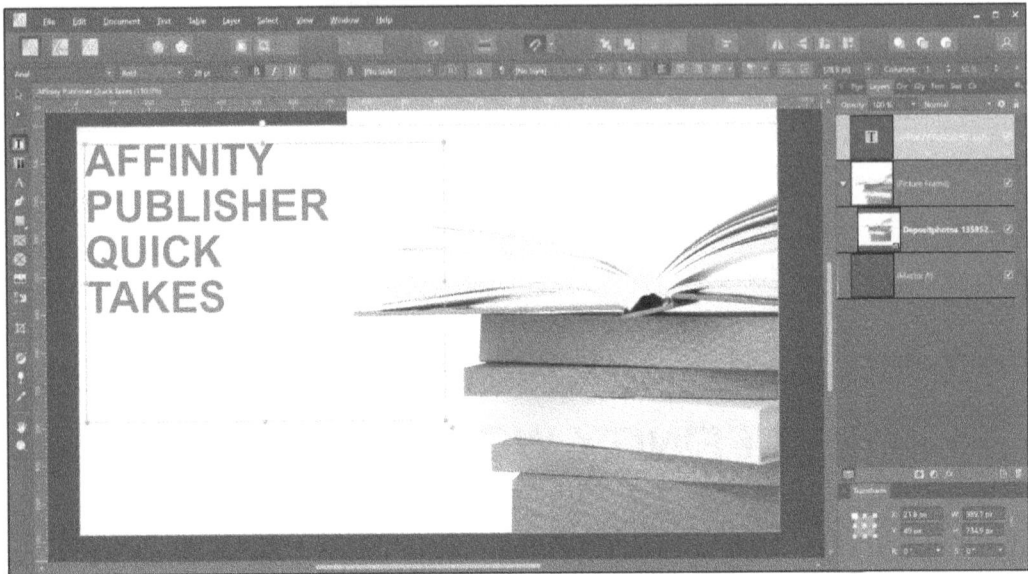

This is a simple image I put together in Affinity Publisher for the video course *Affinity Publisher Quick Takes.*

In the center is the image I created.

On the left-hand side of the workspace you can see a number of small icons like the ones in the screenshot below which each correspond to a different tool available to you in Publisher:

These icons will always be there by default when you have a project open and we are going to use them a lot throughout this book.

When I work on image-heavy projects like ads or covers that is all I have on the left-hand side. (For print layouts I put a number of my often-used studios over there, but not for image-heavy projects. I want as much of my screen space for my design as I can get.)

Along the top of the workspace are options that will change depending upon the tool you have selected on the left-hand side. I may sometimes refer to this as the dynamic toolbar.

Here are a few that are visible when I have the Artistic Text Tool (the capital A) selected.

There are dropdowns there for font, font style, and font size as well as options to click on for bolded, italicized, and underlined text.

A lot of the text-based work and image alignment we do will be done using these top options.

The bold and italic options will only be available if the font you choose has those versions. Unlike when working in Microsoft Word not all fonts you choose will have a bold or italic option. On the other hand, some fonts will have multiple "bold" weights to choose from. In general in Affinity I use the dropdown that says "Regular" to see the available weights for the font I'm using rather than clicking on the B for bold.

Okay. Moving on.

On the right-hand side of the workspace are where I place what Affinity calls studios. I think of them as task panes devoted to specific topics and there are a number of them that I like to keep open for quick use.

Studios can be opened or closed using the View option in the top menu. Go to View->Studio to see your list of available studios.

Those that are already open will show with a checkmark next to the name. Here you can see, for example, that the Character, Color, and Glyph Browser studios are already open but the Anchor, Assets, Constraints, and other listed studios are not.

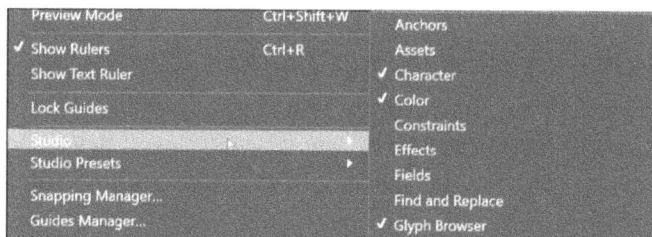

To add a studio to the workspace, click on its name in the dropdown menu. A studio that you open is going to open on top of your workspace in a separate dialogue box. You can left-click and drag on that dialogue box to dock it to the left or right side of the workspace.

By default Affinity has studios docked on the top-left as well as the top, middle, and bottom right. As you can see, for design work I dock most of my studios in the top right corner and then move between them by clicking on the tabs at the top of the section.

When a dialogue box is in a position where it can be docked, you should see a light blue highlight. You can then release the left-click and it should stay in that position. When you drag a newly-opened studio dialogue box to a position where there already is one, it will look like a file tab at the top. Drag to the left or right to position the studio in your desired order relative to the other studios that are already there.

If you have a studio docked that you don't want, you can left-click on it, drag it away from where it's docked, and then click on the X in the top right corner to close it. Or you can go to View->Studio and click on its name in the secondary dropdown menu to uncheck it.

So which studios do I keep open? Let's zoom in on the top section of my workspace to see:

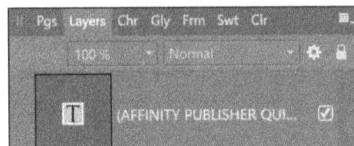

In the image above the Layers studio is currently open, but you can also see the abbreviations for the Pages, Character, Glyph Browser, Text Frame, Swatches, and Color studios. Pages is to the left, the rest are to the right.

I'm going to walk through each one and as I do I recommend that you open and dock it in the same order that I have them so that my screenshots match your workspace. (You don't have to, it'll just make it easier to use this book if we both have the same workspace layout.)

The first tab I have is the Pages studio. By default I believe it is docked on the left-hand side, so left-click on its name and drag to the right-hand side if you want your workspace to look like mine.

The Pages studio will give you a preview of your final document. For example, here is what the image in the workspace would actually look like if I were to export it right now:

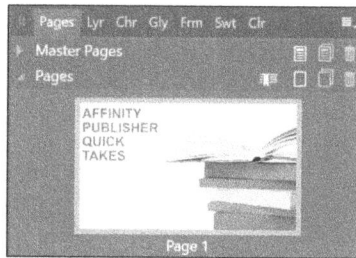

Note that the blue line around the text that's visible in the main workspace is gone and also that the image no longer extends past the edge of the rectangle.

(That gray line around the perimeter is not, however, part of the final image. That's just how it looks when in the Pages studio.)

For design work, I don't use this one all that often, but it's still nice to have pinned to my workspace.

The next studio I have in that top section is the Layers studio.

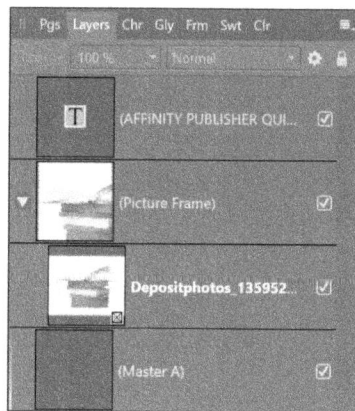

By default I believe it's docked in the middle on the right-hand side, so you'd need to click and drag it up to have the same layout that I use. (I don't like to have any studios in the middle because when you have a lot of layers having those studios there cuts off how many layers you can see at one time.)

The Layers studio is the primary studio I use for design work. This is where you can move items around to make sure that, for example, your text is on top of your image not behind it.

It is also where you can select the correct component to work on. And it's where you can group layers so that they can be moved around together or adjusted together.

Finally, it's where you can turn on or off some image effects and hide or unhide layers. All things that you may want to do as you design your ads.

We will spend a lot more time with this one don't worry.

After that, I have the Character studio.

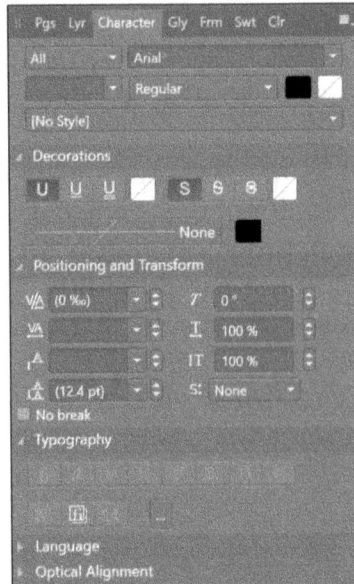

I believe it too is by default in the center on the right-hand side.

This is another one I don't use a lot but it's nice to have handy when I need it. Most of the basic text formatting options are available at the top of the workspace, so you shouldn't need to come here to change the font or font style, although you can.

What it can be useful for is adjusting the kerning or tracking of your text or using all caps or subscripts or superscripts. Basically, more fancy manipulations of your text are found here.

Next I have the Glyph Browser studio.

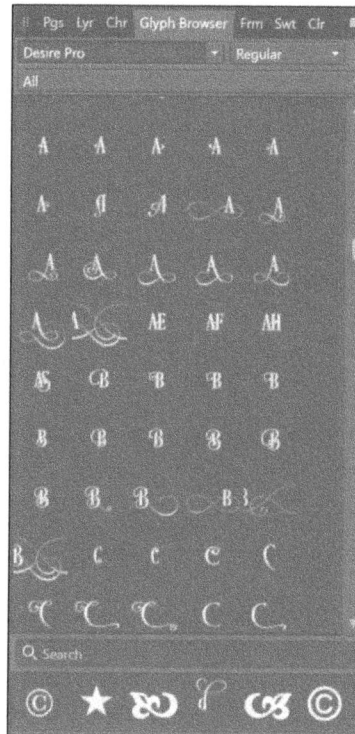

This is not one I believe is open by default so if you want it you'll need to open it via the View menu up top and then dock it. This one is good for when you need to insert design elements that are part of a font or for any font you use that has a lot of variants.

If you look in the main space of the screenshot above you can see that with the Desire Pro font I have seventeen different versions of the capital letter A to choose from, some very basic, some incredibly ornate. (And actually if I scroll up there are ten more choices for the capital letter A, so I have twenty-seven total choices.)

Rather than remember keyboard shortcuts to get each variation, I can just go to the glyph browser studio and double-click on the one I want to use.

In the section below that, you can also see my recently used glyphs for an idea of what else I pull into my designs using the glyph browser.

That star shape is available under the main Wingdings font and is perfect for use in ads where you want to include five stars before the text of a review. This is also how I pull in decorative elements for breaks between text in my ads.

After the glyph browser I have the Text Frame studio.

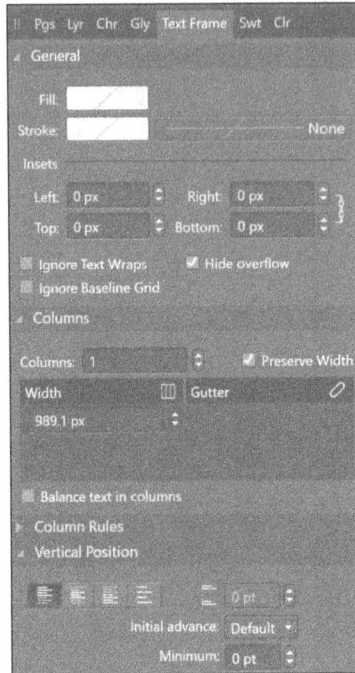

This is another one I don't believe is available by default but that I like to use often enough that I pull it in. It's more for covers than ads, though.

I often use text frames because putting text in a text frame is a good way to have that text aligned within just that frame instead of the entire space you're working in.

After that I have the Swatches studio.

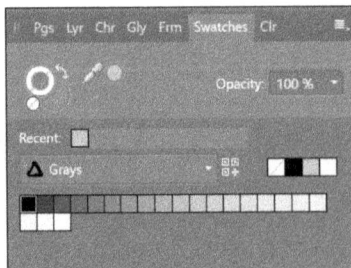

That one is in the top right section by default I believe, so it's just a matter of moving it one to the left past the Color studio. (Left-click, drag, release when in position.)

The Swatches studio is the easiest way to change a color element to black or white. Just click on the swatch square for that color after you've selected whatever it is you need to change.

You can also see there that it shows your current filler color (the filled-in circle) and current outline color (the doughnut shape) at the top. Whichever one of those two is displaying on top is the one that's currently available to use. Click on the other to bring it to the forefront.

A white circle with a red line through it means no color.

You can always change one or the other back to no color using the small white circle with a line through it at the bottom left corner of the two options.

The Swatches studio also allows you to use the eyedropper to select a color from your image. You do have to then double-click on that color to apply it as either the fill color or border color, whichever is currently selected.

Also, once you're working with your document and have used various colors, the Recent section will show square swatches for all colors you've used in the document. This makes it easy to use the same color on multiple components.

The final studio I have in the top right section is the Color studio, which is located there by default. This is the studio that lets you really get wild with colors.

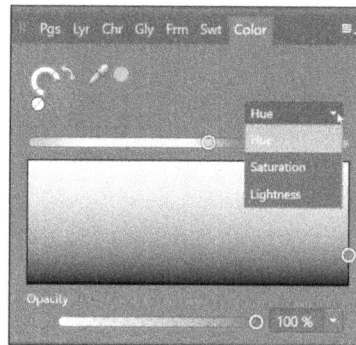

In the default view, you can click on that colored rainbow to choose a general color and then click below to choose any of a range of variations on that color. Or you can change the dropdown to Saturation or Lightness to see the colors presented in a different layout.

You can also adjust the opacity of a color. The lower the opacity the more you can see what's behind it.

This is also where I will double-click on the circle with my current color to bring up the color chooser if I have specific color values I want to use.

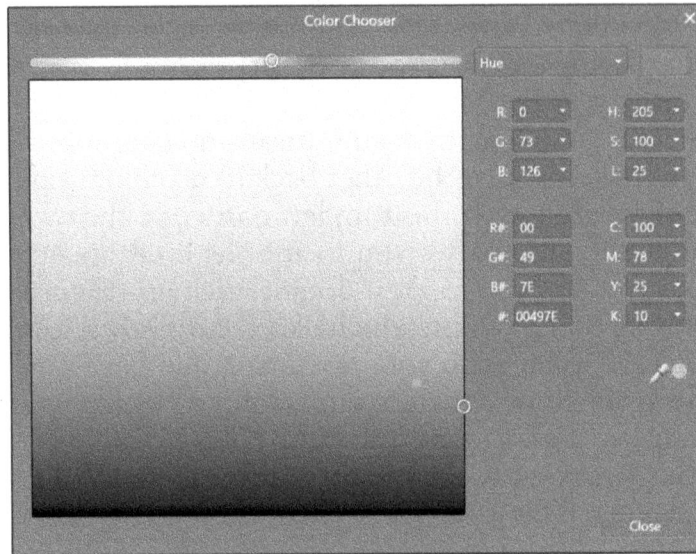

For example, I've found a bright yellow that I like to use for covers and advertisements that displays well and isn't too green or too pale, so I always just input its values using the color chooser when I need to use it.

The Color Chooser is also where you can find the color wheel we discussed earlier.

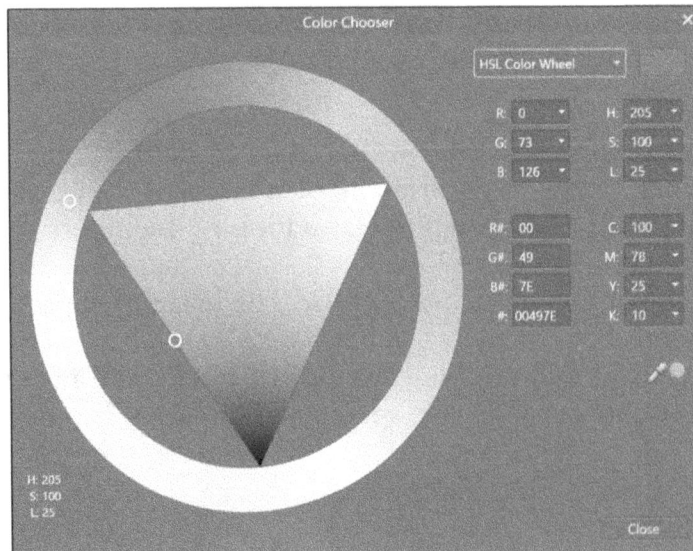

Remember how I said you can draw a line across the circle to find a complementary color to the one you're using? This is where you would do so visually. Just mentally draw a line across from your current color and then click.

Affinity also has studios available in the default view that I don't use. It looks like they start with the Stroke studio in the top right and the Paragraph and Text Styles studios in the middle right.

If you don't want them there, you can left-click and drag each one out to the middle of your workspace and then click on the X in the top right corner to close them. Same for the Assets and Stock studios on the left-hand side.

That leaves us with the bottom right-hand section. The only studio I keep down there is the Transform studio.

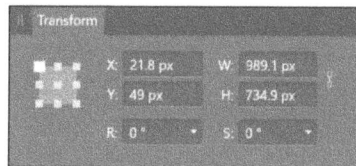

This one is very important. It's where you can see the relative position of an object within the workspace and also the overall dimensions of that object. I will often go to this studio to adjust the size of an image proportionately.

Affinity appears to also by default have the History and Navigator studios here. I rarely if ever use either one. You can leave them there if you want or remove them. Up to you. We won't use them here but you may see them in some of my screenshots just because I didn't remove them before I took my screenshots.

Okay, so that's my set-up. As you learn Affinity you will find the layout that works best for you.

Once you arrange your studios to your liking, I recommend that you save that set-up as a Preset.

To do so, go to View->Studio Presets->Add Preset and type in a name for your preset and then click OK.

Once you've done that, you can always go back to that layout by going to View->Studio Presets and then clicking on the name for your preset under the secondary dropdown menu. So don't be afraid to move things around and experiment a bit. As long as you've saved your layout as a preset, it's always going to be there to go back to.

Let's say you have a preset and then you change your layout and like it better. To save over that existing preset, just act as if you're creating a new preset by choosing Add Preset and give it the exact same name as your old preset. That will overwrite the old layout with your new one.

I love presets, because they let me move back and forth between the very different sets of tools that I use for print interior layouts and ad and cover design.

Finally, to go back to Affinity's default arrangement, I believe you can use View->Studio->Reset Studio. (That's the layout I was talking from when I said that I think that Affinity is by default laid out X way, but I've been working with my presets so long I don't want to swear to it.)

Alright then. Now that we have our workspace arranged, it's time for our first project, which is to take an existing ebook cover image and create an image to upload for use in an Amazon A+ Content Standard Comparison Chart module.

COVER IMAGE FOR USE IN AN AMAZON A+ COMPARISON CHART

One of the issues I've run into on Amazon is that they list my large print books in the same section as the regular-sized print books, which means that someone has to be fairly savvy to find the large print edition of a book. Since with my cozies I assume those are my older readers, I don't want them to have to go through that kind of effort to find the next book in the series.

To get around this issue I leverage Amazon's A+ Content Standard Comparison Chart module. It allows me to provide an image of each book cover, a link to that book, and then random information that I provide to justify the use of the comparison chart module.

Here is an example:

Available Formats	A Dead Man and Doggie Delights	A Crazy Cat Lady and Canine Crunchies	A Buried Body and Barkery Bites	A Missing Mom and Mutt Munchies	A Sabotaged Celebration and Salmon Snaps	A Poisoned Past and Puppermints
	Ebook, Paperback, Large Print Paperback, Large Print Hard Cover	Ebook, Paperback, Large Print Paperback, Large Print Hard Cover	Ebook, Paperback, Large Print Paperback, Large Print Hard Cover	Ebook, Paperback, Large Print Paperback, Large Print Hard Cover	Ebook, Paperback, Large Print Paperback, Large Print Hard Cover	Ebook, Paperback, Large Print Paperback, Large Print Hard Cover

Each of the titles there is a hyperlink to that edition of the book. I list the various formats just because I have to list at least one piece of information in order to use the comparison chart.

Easy enough to do and it solves my problem.

But the image specifications that Amazon lists are not in line with standard cover dimensions. If you go into the A+ Content Manager and you click on Standard Comparison Chart for your module, you'll see this:

Note that the image it wants you to upload is 150:300. That's a 1:2 ratio whereas most covers are a 1:1.6 ratio. Which means that you can't just try to upload your cover, you have to create a modified JPG file for upload.

Let's do that now. It's good practice for working with images in Affinity Publisher.

First things first, open Affinity Publisher, close out any notices about new versions, and then click on New Document in the dialogue box or go to File->New if you've already closed that out.

This will bring up the New Document dialogue box. Click on the web option at the top and then click on one of the listed layouts below that.

On the right-hand side, make sure the page orientation is set to portrait and change the Page Width and Page Height values to 150 and 300 respectively. Here's an example where I've done that with arrows pointing to the respective values:

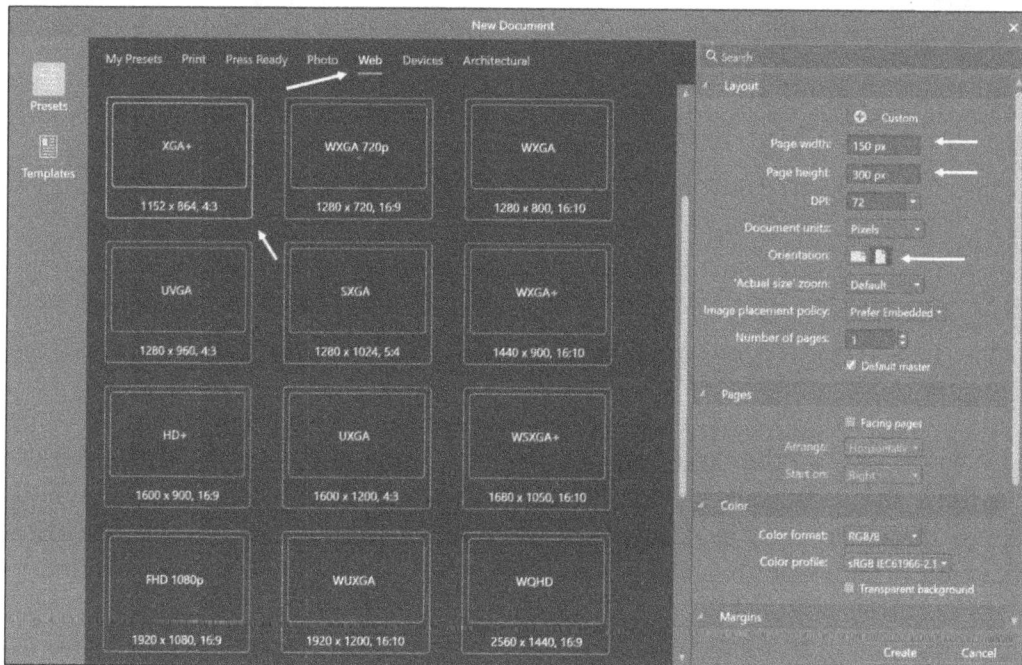

A DPI of 72 and RGB/8 for the color format should be fine.

You can up the DPI if you want. I have mine set to 96 for some reason and some of the templates in the web section use 144. For what we're doing here as long as your setting is at least 72, it should work.

(I'm not going to have you create a preset for this one, because it's better for you to work from the final file we're going to create when you need additional images. That will ensure that all of your images are the exact same size. If you don't know what I'm talking about right now, don't worry, we'll cover it later.)

Okay. Once you've changed those settings, click Create.

You should end up with a workspace that looks something like this:

The Layers studio on the right has just one layer, Master A, and the main workspace shows the blank canvas we asked Affinity to create that's 150 by 300 pixels. You can see those dimensions by looking at the W and H values in the Transform studio in the bottom right corner.

Very exciting. (Or not.)

I'm now going to walk you through two separate ways to place the cover image into your document. (Note: This will work for any image you want to use, not just your cover.)

But first, before we go any further, make sure that you have snapping enabled. It's under the dropdown at the top of the screen that has a horseshoe-shaped magnet. Click on that icon and make sure that the Enable Snapping checkbox is checked.

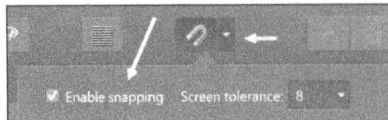

Once snapping is enabled, Affinity will show you red and green lines when you drag your elements around and they align with either other elements in your layout or with the edges of your canvas.

Using these lines is the easiest way to draw out a frame or image to the proper size and to move it around within your workspace and ensure it's aligned or centered.

Okay. Let's place your cover image now.

Option one is to place your cover directly onto the workspace. To do that, go to the left-hand side of the workspace and click on the icon that looks like a painting of a landscape. If you hold your mouse over it, you will see that it is called the Place Image Tool.

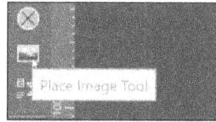

Clicking on that icon will bring up an Open dialogue box. Navigate to where you have your cover saved and select it. Once you've done that, click on Open at the bottom of the dialogue box.

Next you want to left-click on the edge of your workspace about a little over midway up on the left-hand side. Hold that left-click as you drag down and to the right. As you do so, the cover should appear in the white space and increase in size.

Drag all the way to the bottom of the white space. You should see a red line appear across the bottom of the white space when the bottom of the cover aligns to the bottom of the white space.

If you go too far, just move back up until you see that red line. Release the left-click.

When you're done, unless you're a genius at judging dimensions, you should have a cover image that is aligned along the left-hand side of the white space and along the bottom of the white space, but is not yet aligned to the right of the white space. Like so:

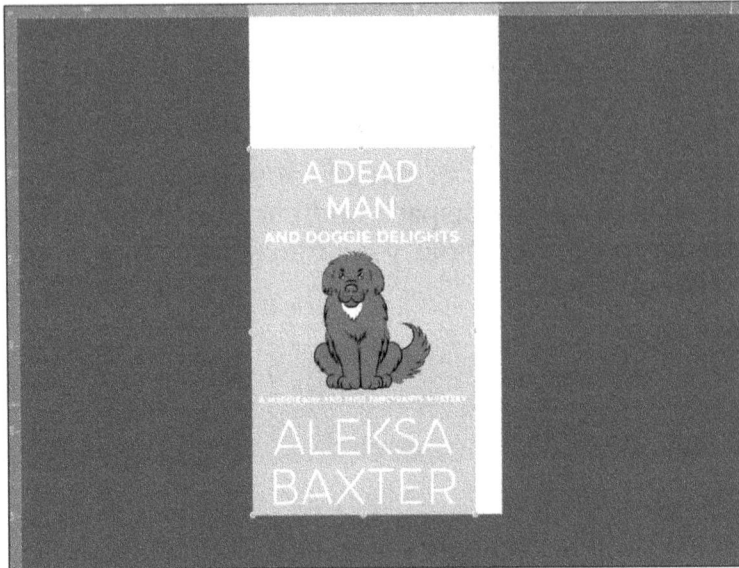

To fix this, click on the blue circle in the top right corner of the cover image and drag at an angle until the cover entirely fills the white space.

When you hit the edge of the white space on the right-hand side you should see a green line appear. Release your left-click.

You should end up with something like this that has your cover at the bottom and filling the space completely from left to right but with white space remaining above:

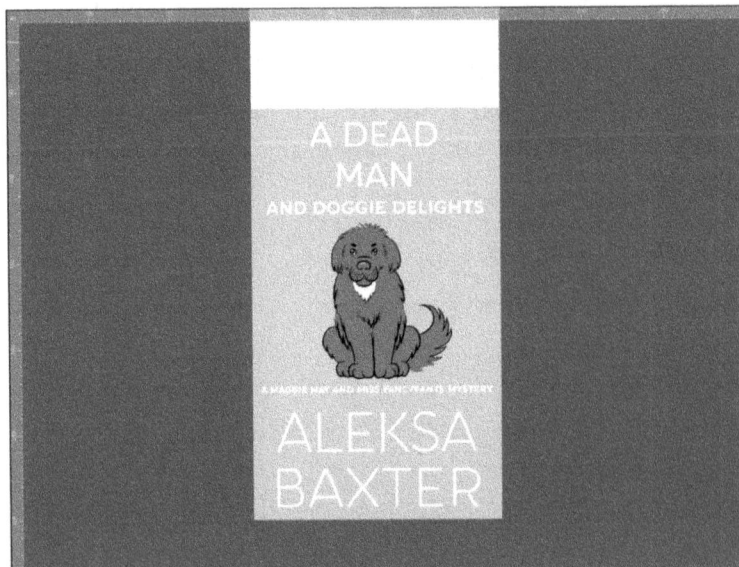

It should not go past the edges of your canvas.

And that's it. You're done. All you need to do is export as a JPG image and save the file so you can use it again.

Options two is to use a Picture Frame first and then drop the cover into the picture frame.

By using a picture frame and then swapping out your image (which we'll cover in a moment) you can ensure that your A+ Content images will always be the same size.

If you're writing fiction and using standard print and ebook dimensions, you probably won't need to do that. You can just use the ebook cover and click and drag on each edge until you see the green and red lines along the edges like we just discussed. That should result in same-sized images each time as long as your ebook covers are all the same dimension and you line them up along the left, bottom, and right sides.

But I do use a picture frame. For two reasons.

First, because most of my non-fiction books are not in standard ebook dimensions and I want to display the print covers in my A+ content not the ebook covers.

The easiest way to do so is by using the PDF I create for the print cover. But that requires sizing the image so that the small excess along the edges of the print template is trimmed away.

Because that's not an exact adjustment, if I did it freehand I'd end up with slightly different image sizes each time. (Ask me how I know...)

The other reason is because some of my older ebook covers were created at a different dimension than my newer ones. Using a picture frame ensures that I'm always going to be creating an image for my A+ content that is the same size.

Okay. That was a lot of talking that probably sounded confusing. Let's go do an example and you'll see what I mean.

If you don't have a print template of your cover, just follow along here and keep it in mind for later.

First, we need to go back to the plain white canvas from before.

If you were following along with me in the first step and so currently have a copy of your cover in your workspace, go to the Layers studio, right-click on the layer that contains the image of your cover, and choose Delete from the dropdown menu.

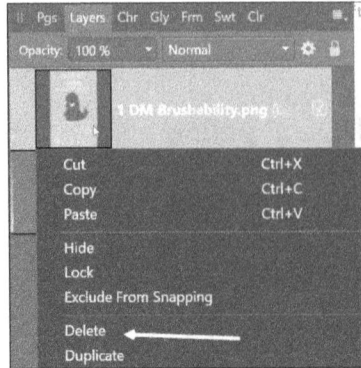

That will remove that layer and take you back to the blank canvas we had before. Alternatively, you can also use Ctrl + Z to Undo back to before the point where you inserted your cover image. Either way, you should be back to a blank canvas before the next step.

Now go back to the left-hand set of icons we used before but this time click on the Picture Frame Rectangle Tool. It's the rectangular image with an X across it that's, at least for me, the eighth one down if you start counting from the black arrow for the Move Tool option.

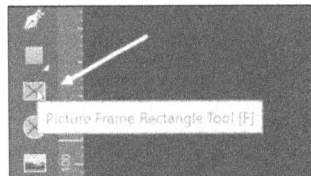

Once you've selected the picture frame tool, left-click and drag from the edge of the white space like you did before when you were inserting your cover. This time when you do so it will form a rectangle with an X in it.

You want the shape you create to be aligned along the left, bottom, and right of the white space and to be the approximate shape of a book cover. If it isn't, you can click on the blue circles along the perimeter of the rectangle and drag each line until it is aligned with the edge and your image is the correct proportions or thereabouts.

When I do this for a 7.5 x 9.25 inch print cover, I end up with something like this:

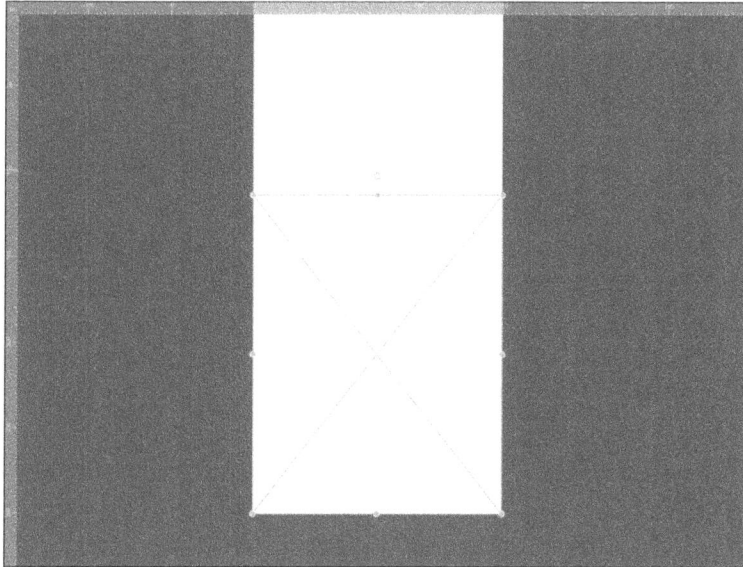

Now it's time to place an image in that frame.

To do so, click on the Place Image Tool that we used before (that looks like a landscape drawing), navigate to the image you want to use, and select it.

Affinity should automatically insert the image into your picture frame as long as you didn't click away from the picture frame in the interim.

Here I've place a PDF of the paperback cover that was the KDP cover version for one of my non-fiction titles.

I prefer to use the KDP version because it's just the cover, there's no extra white space around it like with IngramSpark covers, but either one will work just fine because all that will show in the final image is what's inside the frame, as you can see above.

I inserted the full cover, but you can see that it's cut off. It actually extends to the right and left, but because we're using a picture frame those portions of the image outside of the frame are not visible to us.

If I'd placed the image directly without using that frame the whole image would show in my workspace (we'll see an example of that later), but still would not show in my final exported image. In a situation like that, you can see what would export by going to the Pages studio. I personally find that hard to work with, so I tend to use picture frames a lot.

Like we're doing here. So we have the picture frame and we have the image that's been inserted into it, but we're seeing the wrong part of the image right now.

The next step is to move the image we inserted so that we're seeing the front cover in the frame.

There are two ways to do this. One is to left-click and drag from the center of the four arrows that should be visible in the center of the image.

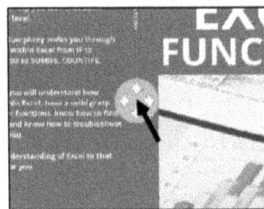

The other is to go to the image layer first in the Layers studio, like here:

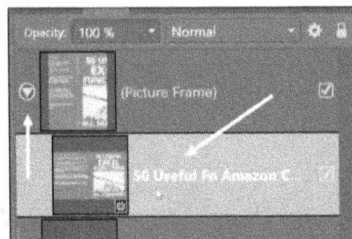

And then click and drag the image like any other object. Use the Move Tool to be able to click anywhere on the image. Otherwise click from the perimeter.

This is what I get initially when I move my cover around:

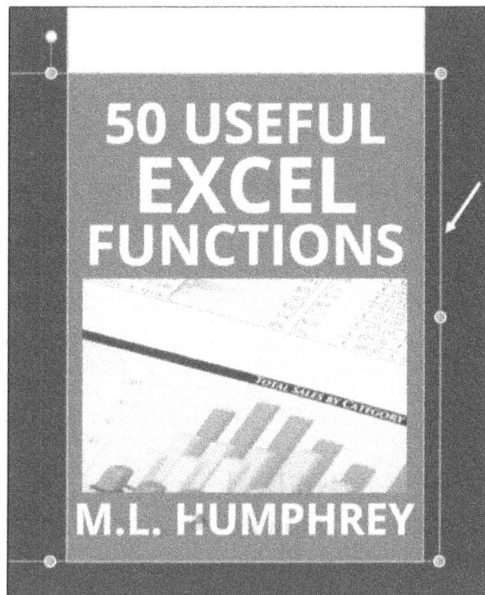

You can see the blue border that represents the border of the image I'm working with, but note how only the portion of the image that's in the picture frame is visible in the workspace.

Now, I was guesstimating the size of the picture frame when I inserted it and you likely will be too. And chances are you won't get it right the first time around.

For example, here I'm seeing too much of the colored background on the top and bottom. I'd prefer it was about the same amount as we're seeing on the left and right sides. Which means I need to adjust the picture frame so that it's a little shorter.

To do so, I can go to the Layers studio and click on the layer for the picture frame. (Remember that we're currently clicked onto the image that's indented below that.)

Clicking on the picture frame ensures that any edits are going to be made to the picture frame, not the image it contains.

Once you've done that, go back to the workspace, click on the blue circles along the edge of the frame and drag them to adjust the frame to the size you want.

In my case, I click on the blue circle at the top and drag downward to make my text frame shorter.

Since I know I'm going to need to reposition my image to center it again in my resized picture frame, I bring the edge of the picture frame almost down to the top line of text in the cover:

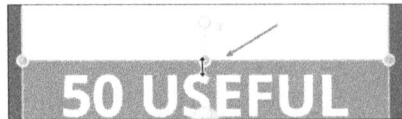

Once my picture frame is resized, I can once more click and drag to center the cover in the newly-resized picture frame.

Sometimes you'll have to move back and forth between the frame and the image a few times to get it right. You may even need to resize the image at some point.

(To resize the image you can usually use the slider below the image. Either that or select the image layer in the Layers studio and then click and drag the image from the corner or change its size in the Transform studio with Lock Aspect Ratio on.)

Also, remember that Ctrl + Z, Undo, does work in Affinity Publisher.

So if you accidentally adjust the picture frame instead of the picture or the picture instead of the picture frame, just use Ctrl + Z to undo and then go back and click on the appropriate layer in the Layers studio before you try again.

(This can come in handy, too, when Affinity decides to change both the picture frame and the underlying image at the same time. Usually that happens if you don't have the picture frame layer expanded in the Layers studio at the time you try to change its size.)

Anyway. Ultimately after I made my adjustments I ended up with this:

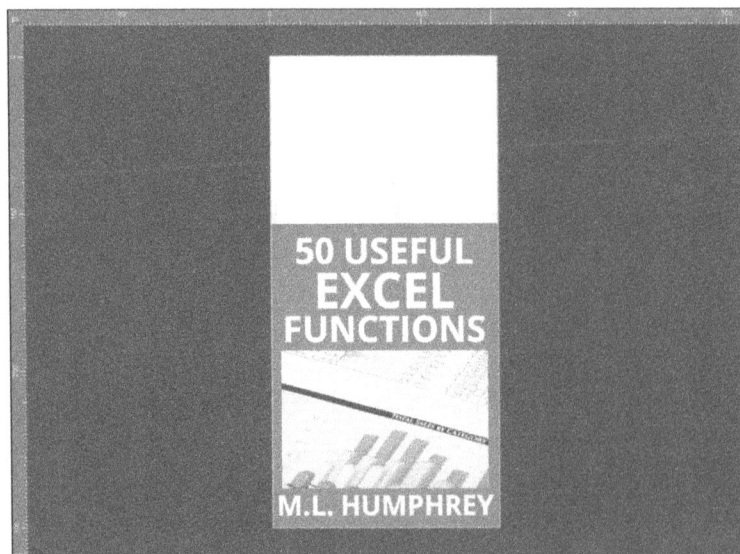

That works.

It's a subtle difference, but you can see that the portion of the cover on the top and bottom that is a solid color is now smaller and more in proportion to the sides. This now looks more like the actual print cover does when the book is printed.

Whichever of the above methods you use, once you're done you're going to want to export the image as a JPG file. (See the later chapter for how to export images.) You can then upload it to Amazon and it will look like this:

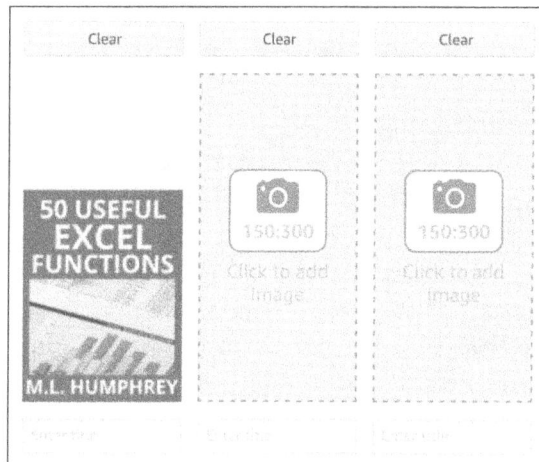

Note how the white space above the cover simply disappears and it looks like you just uploaded your cover and nothing else.

Perfect.

Also, for this one, save the final file for future use. (File->Save)

The reason you want to save a copy of the file and use it again is because once you've set up your first comparison content file, it's very, very easy to swap in a new cover without having to redo all the work we just did.

And it's better to swap out the covers if they're the same dimensions because that will ensure that the A+ content image dimensions are exactly the same each time.

Let me show you how to do that now.

With your final file open, go to Document->Resource Manager. This will bring up the Resource Manager dialogue box which will show you all of the images that are in your document.

In this case, we just have the one.

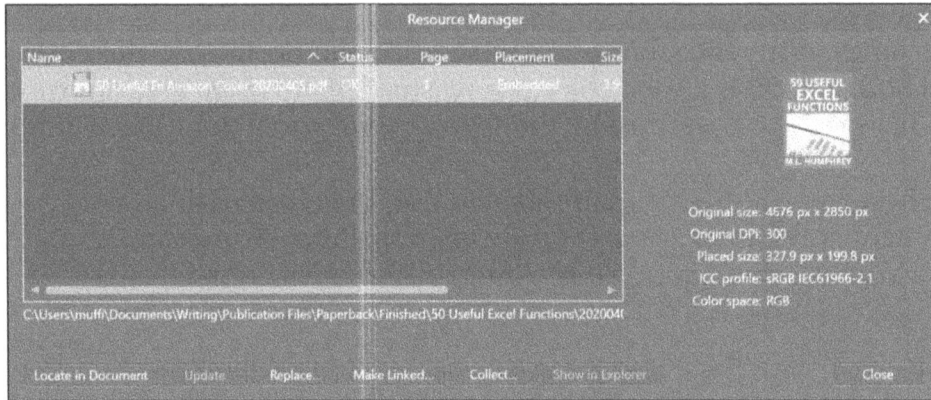

Click on that listing for the image like I have above—it will highlight in blue—and then click on Replace at the bottom of the dialogue box.

In the Open dialogue box that appears, navigate to where the next cover image you want to use is saved, select it, and choose Open.

Your other option is to click on the image layer and then use the Replace Image option in the dynamic menu up top. It should be visible when the Move Tool or Picture Frame Tool is selected.

Either option will bring in that replacement image in the exact same location as the one that you used previously. For ebook covers, that should be all you have to do. They're generally going to be the exact same dimensions so there's no adjustment to be made.

For print covers, you will likely need to move the cover image right or left because the different spine widths for print books make the files different sizes which means Affinity will place them differently.

If you do need to make an adjustment when working with a picture frame, be sure to make it to the *image* layer not the *picture frame* layer. The picture frame layer is what keeps everything looking uniform and the same size. If you change the picture frame then your images will not match up when they're side-by-side.

Also, assuming the two images were created the same way, try to limit your adjustments to moving the image left or right. If you resize the new image, it may look wrong when set next to the old image because, for example, the text will be bigger or smaller between the two images.

If you do find yourself having to resize your second image, then you may want to consider going back and redoing your first one so that they match in terms of overall size and relative size.

This is, of course, assuming the source files were the same general dimensions.

(It won't normally be that big of an issue and you're probably going to be dealing with ebook covers so it shouldn't be any issue at all, but it might happen so I wanted to cover it just in case.)

Okay. Done. That was how to create the 150:300 image you need for an Amazon A+ Content Comparison Chart. Now on to something more custom. Let's talk about how to create an image that shows all of your book covers for use on an A+ Content page, FB banner, or website banner.

BANNER IMAGE CONTAINING MULTIPLE BOOK COVERS

The example we're going to do here is for A+ Content, but honestly, change the dimensions up and it could be for a Facebook banner or a webpage banner or any of a number of other advertising options.

What we're going to create is something that looks like this:

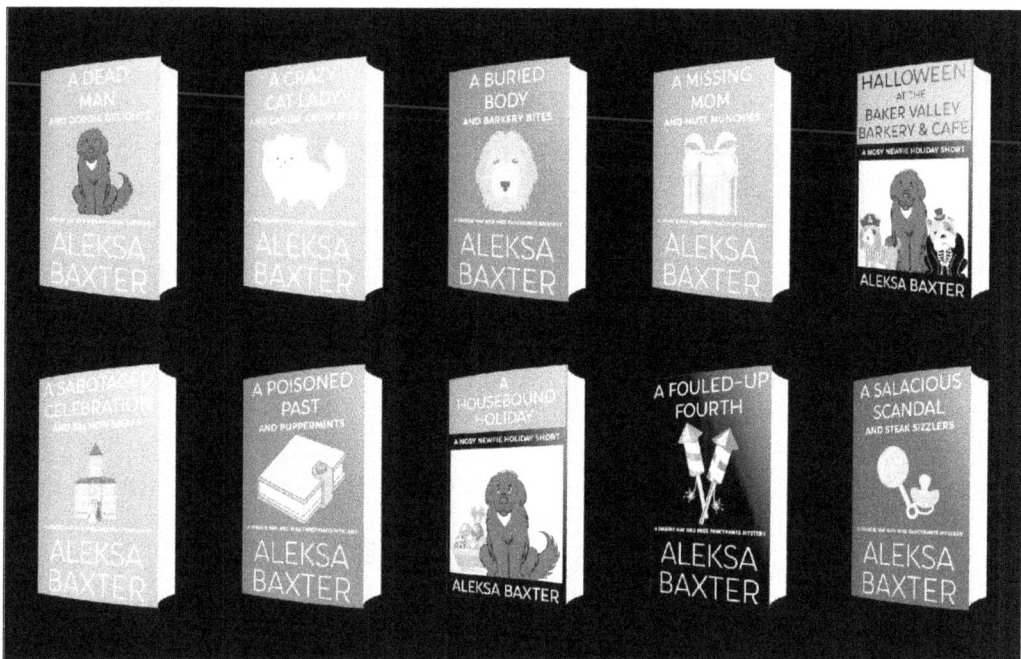

This is probably far more complex than most authors will need, but doing one with this many covers allows me to show you a few extra tricks you can use in Affinity. And the skills we're going to cover here will work as well for three covers as they do for ten.

* * *

First things first, where can you get the three-dimensional images for your covers?

If you're really lucky your cover designer provided you with one. And, even better, it was a PNG file with a transparent background.

I have one that my cover designer provided that was a JPG file with a white background that makes it very challenging to use in a lot of settings. So if, like me and many others, you are not lucky enough to have a usable file from your cover designer, you have a couple of other options.

Option two is to use Book Brush (https://bookbrush.com) to create a three-dimensional cover. Last I checked they offered fifteen free downloads, so you could easily get enough of your covers done that way to create what we're going to do here for free. And they're also reasonably priced if you have more covers than that.

Option three is to use Affinity *Photo*. If you have Affinity Photo then you can go to Covervault (https://covervault.com) and download one of their free book mockups. For this example I used the 5.5 x 8.5 Standing Paperback Book Mockup.

In Affinity Photo change your Preferences so that "Import PSD smart objects where possible" is checked. This will allow you to open most mockup templates which are usually created as PSD files for Photoshop.

Once you open the mockup file in Affinity Photo it's just a matter of double-clicking on the embedded document layer for the cover where you can then insert the cover image using File->Place which is very much like using the Place Image Tool in Publisher.

If the image doesn't fit the space perfectly, you may also need to use the Flood Fill Tool on the left-hand side (looks like a paint bucket) to fill in the background with your cover color. Or you'll need to stretch the cover a bit to fit the space.

From here on out, I'm going to assume that you've used one of the above options and that you have three-dimensional versions of your covers to work with. If you don't, you can do this with two-dimensional covers instead.

* * *

For this project, we're going to once more use picture frames and work with replacing images, but we're also going to learn how to select multiple layers, group layers, duplicate layers, align objects, and add a colored background in Publisher.

Okay. First things first, we need a new document to work in. The A+ Content module I use for this is 970 pixels by 600 pixels.

So go to File->New, choose one of the Web presets, and modify the pixel size to 970 by 600. 72 DPI is fine. It should be landscape. And RGB/8 is fine for the color. This will give you a big white rectangle in your workspace.

Next we need to add a colored background.

To do this, you want the Rectangle Tool which is the blue-colored square icon about seven down on the left-hand side of the workspace. We're just going to click on the blue square, but if you click on the little white arrow in the bottom right corner you can see all sorts of other shapes that are available in Affinity.

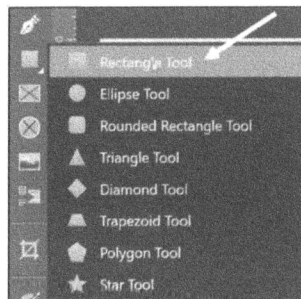

Click on the Rectangle Tool, then left-click in a corner of the white canvas in your workspace and hold that left-click down as you drag at a diagonal to the opposite corner. Your goal is to cover the entire canvas with this rectangle. You should see the green and red snapping lines when you hit the edge of the canvas.

If you let up on the left-click without reaching the edges or go too far, you can left-click on the blue circles around the perimeter and drag each edge into alignment separately.

Depending on what color you had as your Fill color it may not look like you changed much. Mine is a light gray so it really isn't noticeable. But if you look in the Layers studio you will now see that you have a Rectangle layer in addition to your Master layer.

Let's go ahead and make our rectangle black instead.

Above the workspace in the dynamic menu area, you should see a Fill option with a small rounded rectangle next to it that shows the same color as the rectangle you just drew. Click on that rounded rectangle to open a dropdown dialogue box with color options.

Mine opened to the Color tab, but since I just want a black background, I am going to click on the Swatches tab, and then the square swatch for black. That will turn my rectangle in my workspace into a solid black rectangle instead of light gray like it was before.

The Swatches tab is the best option for black, grays, or white. The Color tab is better for actual colors as you can see with the rainbow of options and then the various iterations of those colors that show below in the screenshot above.

Click on the rainbow to select the color you want and then click anywhere in that large rectangular space to select the specific shade of the color.

Now that our background is in place we're ready to add our cover images.

I like to do this with picture frames so that everything is the same size and I don't have to worry about the perimeter of two images overlapping. This is especially true with 3D covers which often come with extraneous space around the actual cover. By using a picture frame, only the cover portion of the image that I place in the frame will show in my design.

Okay. So we need to start with a picture frame. Click on the Picture Frame Rectangle Tool we used before and then left-click and draw a shape on the canvas in your workspace that's about 200 pixels tall by 125 pixels wide.

You should be able to see the dimensions as you click and drag to form your shape. Mine came out to a W of 128.8 and an H of 197.3.

If you want exact measurements, go down to the Transform studio and type those values into your W and H fields like here where I've changed them to 125 and 200:

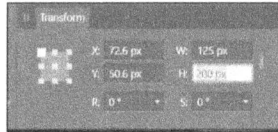

Next, click on the Place Image Tool and go find your first 3D cover.

If you haven't clicked away from the picture frame, it should insert the image directly into your frame, like so:

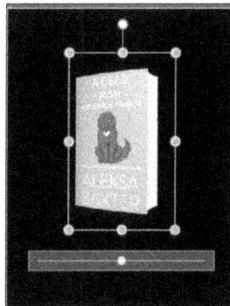

Adjust the position of your cover so that it's centered in the box you created and so that it also fills most of the space.

Remember, you can either use the slider below the image to change its size and click in the center of the four arrows in the center of the image to click and drag to reposition the image, or you can go to the Layers studio and click down to the image layer before trying to move or resize the image like any other element.

If you use the image layer option, you should place a border around the image first (which we're going to do next) so that you can see the borders of the picture frame as you reposition the image.

I'm going to place a border because that's what Affinity will use for alignment with other elements. First, though, I want to hide the black background layer.

I can do that by going to the Layers studio and unchecking the box for that layer.

Once I'm working on a white background, I can then click on the picture frame layer in the Layers studio and in the dynamic menu above the workspace click on the white line with a red slash through it next to Stroke to add a line around the frame by moving the slider for Width to the right until there is a visible frame around my image. Like so:

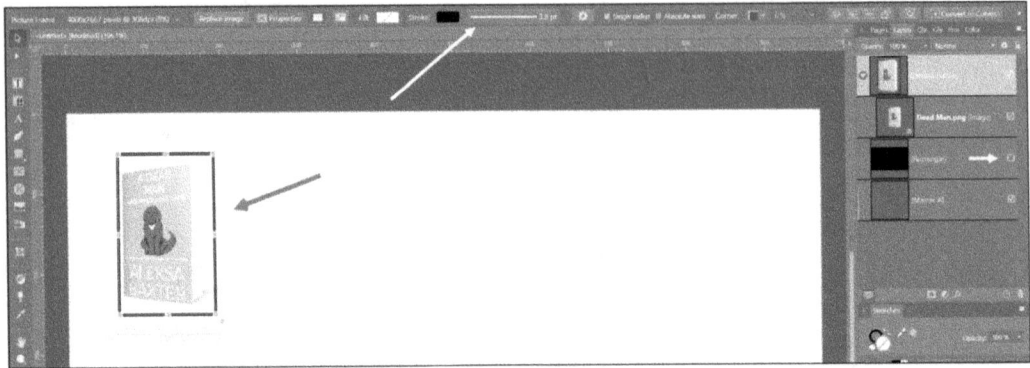

You can see that the width of the line around the frame is now 3.8.

That lets me see the borders of my frame at all times.

After I manually increase the size of the image a bit and also move it around until it is centered top to bottom and side to side, here's what I ultimately end up with:

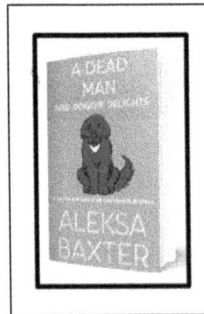

I had to center the image manually because the underlying image does not have the book cover centered. This is an issue you will probably run into with most of the 3D cover templates that are available for free.

The nice thing about using a black border for the picture frame when I have a black background is it's going to blend right in when I turn the background layer back on so I don't have to remove it. In the meantime it will let me see the boundaries Affinity is using for aligning my cover images to one another.

Fortunately, we only needed to do all of that positioning once, because we can just swap in all of the other covers for this one at the end since they're all the exact same size. Which means our next step is to copy the picture frame and cover we just created nine more times.

One fun trick that Affinity does when you copy an object is that if you copy the object and then move it and then make another copy, Affinity will paste *and move* that second copy. Which means that you only have to move the first copy you make, Affinity will space out the other copies for you.

It's maybe best understood in action.

Below what I did is clicked onto the Picture Frame layer in the Layers studio, right-clicked, and chose Duplicate. I then clicked onto the picture frame in my workspace and dragged the duplicated image over so that I had two duplicate images side by side like so:

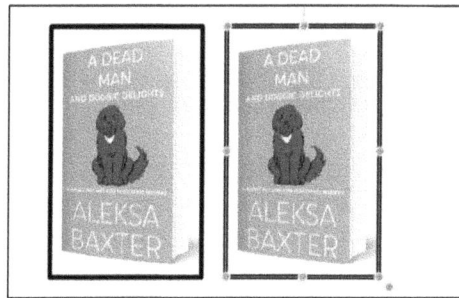

After that I could just right-click and Duplicate that layer in the Layers studio three more times and what I ended up with was five covers in picture frames, all evenly spaced.

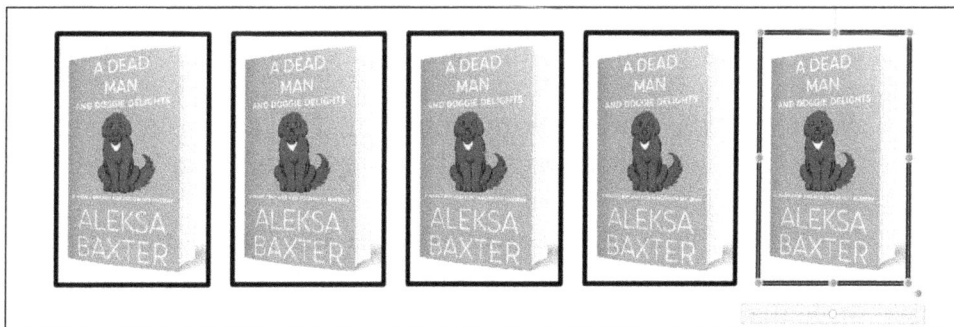

Basically, Affinity saved me a little bit of clicking and dragging for each image I copied.

So that's the first five covers. Rather than repeat that five more times, we can now group those covers and copy the group.

To do so, go to the Layers studio, click on the top or bottommost of the picture frame layers, hold down the shift key, and click on the other end of the range of picture frame layers.

You should see all five of the layers highlighted in blue like this:

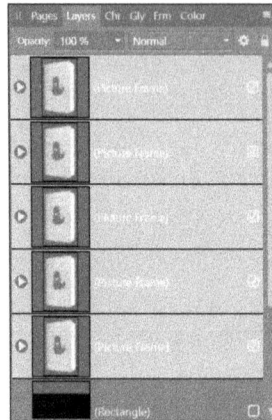

Use Ctrl + G to group them. You could also right-click and choose Group from the dropdown menu, but Ctrl + G is faster and you'll use it often enough it's worth memorizing.

When you group the picture frames, this will create a primary layer called Group in your Layers studio.

You can still click on the arrow next to the Group layer name to expand the group and see each of the individual picture frame layers below it.

If you want to rename the group, you can click on the name (Group) and then type in a new name. For complex projects it probably makes sense to do so. For something like this I don't bother.

The nice thing about grouping objects is you can then move them around together as one item.

You can also resize the entire group together. For example, maybe I want covers that are 250 pixels tall now that I'm looking at this. That would fill out my background better.

Rather than change the height of every one of the five picture frames, I can click onto the group layer in my Layers studio and then go to my canvas and click on the blue circle in any corner and drag at an angle to resize the entire group at once.

(I could click on that Group layer in the Layers studio and change the dimensions in the Transform studio, but I'd need to remember to Lock Aspect Ratio before I did that or my images would skew.)

Here's what I get in my workspace when I select the group and click and drag to resize all of the covers at once:

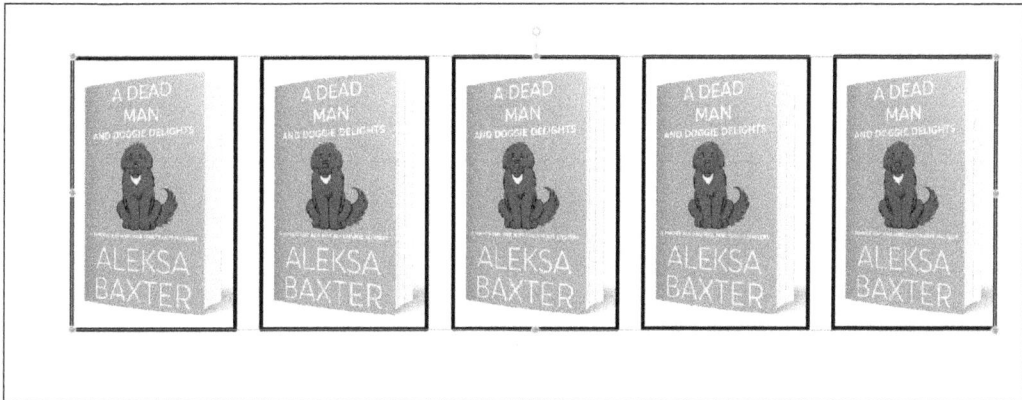

But I still have an issue, which is that the covers are evenly spaced compared to one another but they are not evenly spaced across my canvas. Right now the covers are more to the right side of the canvas than the left.

Also, they need to be spaced apart from one another a little bit more because even centered I'm going to have too much space along the outer edges.

First things first, let's center the group as it exists right now.

To do so, make sure you're clicked on the group layer in the Layers studio and then go to the Alignment option at the top of the workspace, which is a bar with two blue lines coming off the right-hand side. Clicking on that will open the alignment dropdown menu. Under Align Horizontally click on the Align Center option:

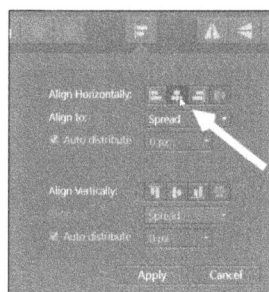

When you do this Affinity will center the entire group on your canvas based upon where the outer edge of the first cover is and where the outer edge of the last cover is.

(This is why using picture frames helps so much because an uneven image may have 25 pixels on the left and 100 on the right so that even though it looks fine on the canvas because that difference blends into the background it won't look right if you try to center it.)

Okay. Anyway. This is what I get when I center my group of five covers:

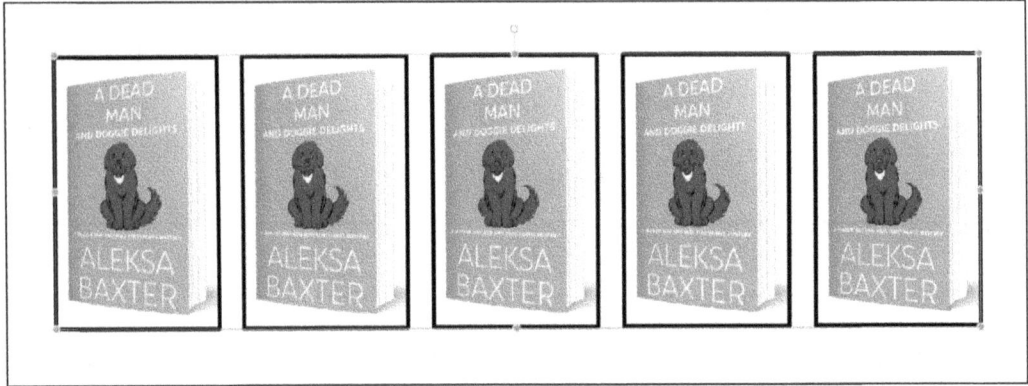

You can see that the amount of white space on the left of the first cover is more than the amount of white space between each of the covers. Which may actually be fine. We're going to end up with some space on the top and bottom and that may actually match up with the space there and look fine.

But let's say I want the covers to be closer to the edge, which means I need to spread them out more. Affinity will space them evenly for me, but I first need to move the covers on the left and right out to where I want the outer edge to be on each side.

To do so, I go to the Layers studio, expand the Group layer, click on the picture frame layer for the left-most cover image, and then go back into the workspace and move that frame to the left until it's where I want it to be. I then do the same for the right-most cover.

(You could technically just move one of the covers, but I prefer to move both because it lets me better establish my outer edges. If I only did one I'd have to mentally adjust where I placed it based upon the fact that I'd be re-centering my group when I was done.)

Okay. So doing that will give you something like this:

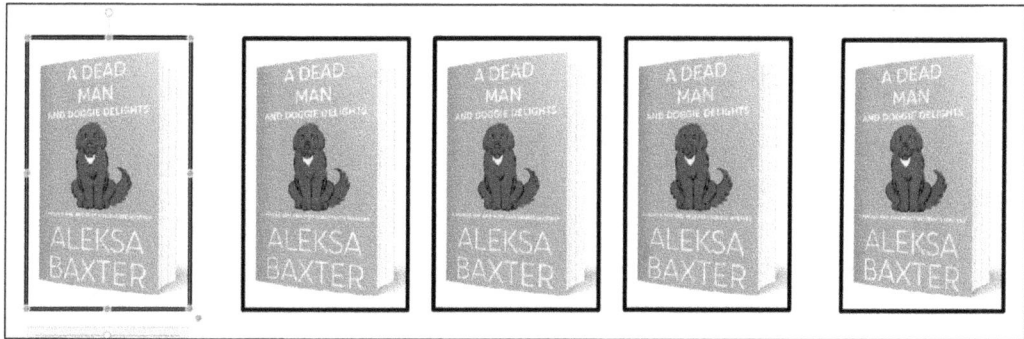

See how there's more space between the first and second frames now? And between the fourth and fifth? But how my first and last covers are closer to the outer edge and have about the same amount of space between their outer edge and edge of my canvas?

Now I need Affinity to evenly space my picture frames across this amount of expanded space.

My first step is to go into the Layers studio and select the layers for all five covers (click on the bottommost one, Shift, click on the topmost one). Next, I go up to the Alignment option once more but this time I choose the Space Vertically option under Align Horizontally. It's the one on the far right.

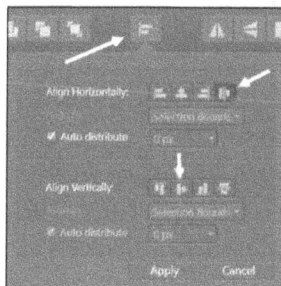

While we're there we can also click on Align Middle under the Align Vertically section just in case when I dragged one of the covers over I also dragged it up or down a little bit.

What that gives me is all five covers spaced out equally between the outer edge of the picture frame for the first cover and the outer edge of the picture frame for the last cover with all of the frames also aligned along the top and bottom edge as well.

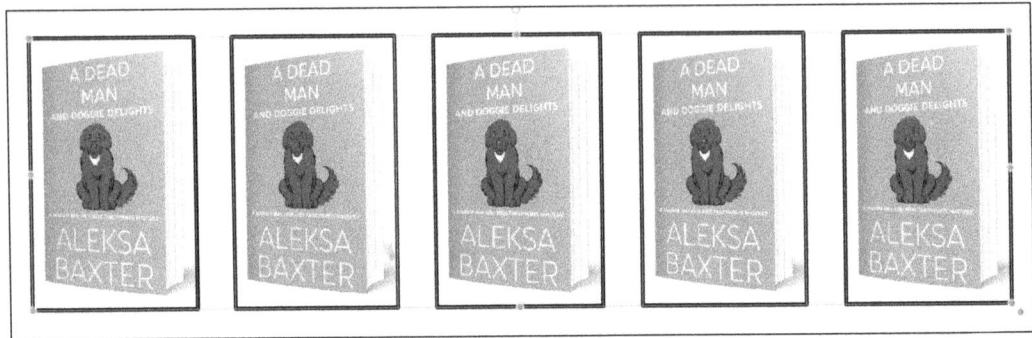

Perfect.

Now that we have our first row of covers set up the way we want them, we just need to duplicate this group to create our second row of covers.

To do so, I go back to the Group layer in the Layers studio, right-click, and choose Duplicate from the dropdown menu. I can then click on the visible covers in the canvas and drag down the duplicated layer so it doesn't overlap the original one.

I could try to manually center and space the two rows, but it's easier to let Affinity do it for me. To do that, select both groups in the Layers studio (using the Ctrl key if they're not next to one another) and then go to the Alignment option at the top of the workspace.

This time we want to Align Center under Align Horizontally but we need to use Spread as the parameter. And then under Align Vertical we can click on Space Vertically and use the auto distribute setting to spread the two rows apart from one another. I chose 32 pixels as a good distance between the two rows.

Next, create a new group from the two row groups in the Layers studio. Go back to the Alignment option and this time choose Align Middle under Align Vertically. That will center the combination of the two rows top to bottom so that they have an equal amount of space above and below the two rows

Turn back on the background layer by checking its box in the Layers studio and you should have something that looks like this:

(The apparent downward versus upward angle of the covers in the two rows is just an optical illusion, because all ten images are the exact same image.)

Okay. All that's left to do is to swap out the covers. One way to do this is with the Resource Manager.

Click on the second cover on the top row and then go to Document->Resource Manager in the top menu.

Because all of the covers are currently the same, there's only one line showing in the resource manager dialogue box. But we can click on the arrow next to that line and it will expand to show all ten instances of that image in the document. Here are the first four showing:

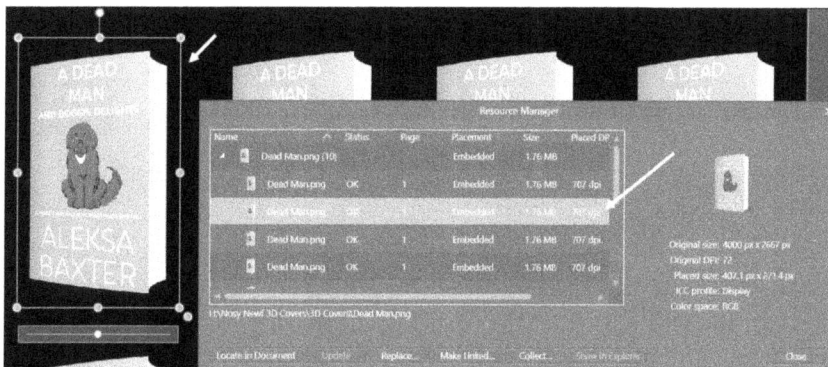

The row that corresponds to the selected image is going to already be highlighted, so just click on Replace and find the second cover that you want to use. Choose Open and Affinity will insert that image into your document in the second cover spot.

Like so:

Your other option is to use the Replace Image option in the dynamic menu at the top of the workspace. It should be visible when the Move Tool or Picture Frame Tool are selected.

Click on the cover you want to replace, click on Replace Image, and then navigate to the replacement image and select it.

Repeat until all of the covers have been replaced.

If you insert the wrong image at any point, Ctrl + Z, Undo, or replacing the image with the correct one is probably your best option instead of trying to drag things around to put them in the right location, because if you move any of the picture frames you'll have to realign your images again.

As you replace each image it will get its own listing in the resource manager. Like so:

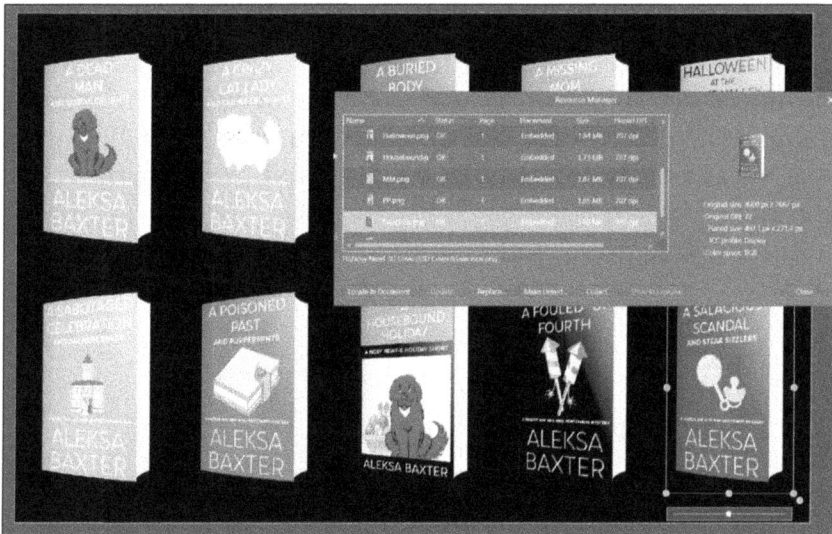

And there you have it. Once you've swapped out all of the covers, you're done.

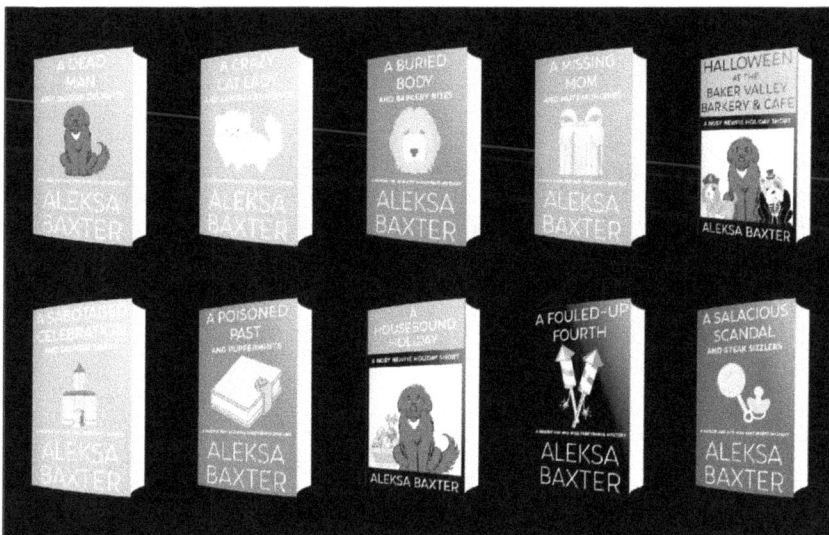

Most people won't have ten covers they want to do this way, but the theory remains the same whether it's three covers or twenty. The only issue is visual balance and which of the A+ modules will work best with the number of covers you do have.

I didn't include text here, but for shorter series, you may want to use part of the banner space to do so because it'll give better balance to the use of the space. After we do the ad creatives you should easily be able to make that adjustment.

And remember that what we covered here can work for website banners, Facebook banners, etc. Basically anything that uses a solid background where you want your cover or other images to be displayed. So don't think this is limited to A+ Content.

Okay, then. Now let's put together some advertisements.

BRIEF AD DISCUSSION

Before we do our first ad, though, I want to take a step back and talk advertising in general for a moment.

Amazon AMS ads were the first ads I ever ran where I could get daily sales at full price. They are still my primary advertising spend for non-fiction because of that.

And what's great about AMS is that it's basically your cover driving clicks. No need to also master the art of the two-hundred-word sales pitch or eye-catching ad creatives.

But at some point, especially on the fiction side, AMS ads aren't enough to drive sales. (For me. YMMV.)

Facebook ads, though, if you can master them (and they don't shut down your account repeatedly, ahem), have tremendous potential to generate sales. And not just on Amazon but on all of the sales platforms. They can also be cheaper to run. At least that's been my experience with free runs.

For example, in 2021 I ran a first-in-series title for free for a couple of months at the end of the year. On FB I was able to get around 10 cents a click for my ads, sometimes as low as 6 cents a click. I could get clicks on AMS, too, but they were more like 30 cents a click.

(Now, one could argue that maybe the resultant sales were equivalent because the people on Amazon were already there to buy books whereas the people on FB maybe weren't, so the Amazon downloads were more likely to result in an immediate read and buy of the next book, but for my money I preferred the results from the FB ads.)

Which makes FB ads a tremendous tool to have when you need them.

But one of the problems with running FB ads is that you have to come up with your own advertising images. And that's not an easy thing to do.

I say this based upon the fact that I've sat through a couple years now of one of those high-priced FB advertising courses where people share their ad images. Some do great at coming up with eye-catching ads. Some do not.

(And trust me, I'm not trying to insult anyone here. Sometimes I miss the boat on my ad images, so this is not me looking down on anyone. Hell, you may look at the ones I'm about to show you and think, "Yeah, look who's talking," which, fair enough. But I will point out that the ads I'm going to use here have been profitable for me on Facebook so they're at least successfully reaching *my* particular audience. Or at least a part of it.)

So what makes a good ad?

At a very high level a good ad is one that attracts *your* type of reader and gets them to buy or download your book.

At a more granular level that requires the ad to convey to your target audience that this is something they want.

You do this through the use of text, images, colors, and overall visual appeal.

Which is all a bunch of gobbledy-gook, right? How do you put that into action? It's like "write a good book and it will sell". Okay. How?

The best advice I can give you is to see what others who are successful with running ads in your particular genre are doing, use that to inform your ads, and then experiment until you find something that works for *your* books.

Also keep in mind that selling your book is about alignment. I don't want to divert away from the focus of this book, but I'm going to give you the ten-second version of this lecture.

It is not enough to have a clicky ad. Your ad needs to align with what the potential customer sees on your book product page, too. And, ideally, with the content of the book.

That means your ad, book description, reviews, price, and category listings all have to tell the same story about what the reader is going to get if they download or buy. And if you want them to read more of your books the book itself has to deliver on the promise of the ad and the product page.

I can definitely get a lot of clicks on an ad with a picture of a hot guy. But that does me no good if I'm actually trying to sell a non-fiction book about organizing your closet. (Not unless I make it clear in the ad how those two connect.)

When an ad doesn't perform you need to go down the entire chain.

If you're not getting clicks, what's wrong with the ad image? If you are getting clicks, but no sales or downloads, where's the disconnect between the ad and the product page? If you're getting sales or downloads but no follow through to the next book, what did you promise to readers but fail to deliver?

Or, how did you get them to download, but fail to excite them enough to read? (I have books on my TBR bookcase that have been there for twenty-five years. Why have those books in all those years never quite interested me enough to actually read them?)

Bottom line is you are going to have to experiment to get that all working together. I can't do that for you. What I am doing here is showing you the mechanics of putting together your ads so that you can easily switch them up until you find what works for your books.

Let's get started with our first one, a FB square ad.

FACEBOOK SQUARE AD USING A BACKGROUND IMAGE

Some of my more successful FB ads have been square ones that leverage an image as the background.

In my case these are for my YA fantasy series that has professionally-designed covers. When I changed from the first set of covers that featured a young woman to object-based covers I was able to continue to use the images from my first set of covers as background in my FB ads.

But what we're going to do here can work with any background image, it doesn't have to be an image that comes from your cover. The key, again, is to convey genre and type of story.

Here's the ad I'm going to build:

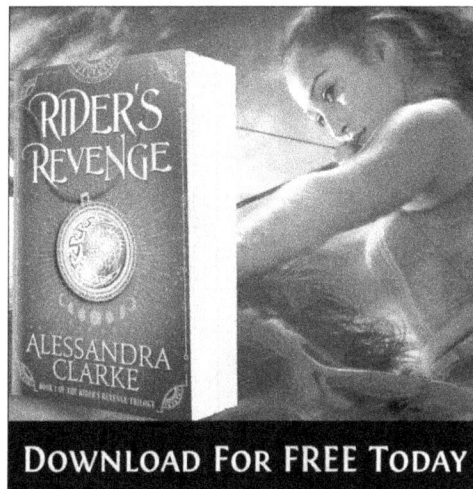

A quick note here: I did not design either of these covers. I do not have this level of skill. But I can leverage the skill that went into creating these covers in my own ads.

This is an ad I used for a free run for my YA fantasy book in February 2021. The cost per click for this ad set came out at 10 to 11 cents per click with a daily spend set to $10 and it was profitable.

It is a very simple ad. It only has four components: the book cover, the background image, the black space at the bottom, and the text in that black space. That's it.

But hopefully it does what it needs to do. Says this is an ad for a book. That the book is about a young woman. That it's a fantasy novel. Probably fantasy adventure with what looks like a horse and a bow involved. And that they can download it for free if they click on the link.

The beauty of an ad like this is that once you create it, there are an infinite number of variations you can design from this base very quickly.

You can change the book, the background image, the text, the color of the black bar at the bottom. You can move the elements around if you need to.

It shouldn't take more than five minutes to have a new ad once you've built the first one. (Whether that new ad is any good is another question, but the mechanics of swapping elements are not time-consuming.)

So let's go create this now in Affinity.

First step is we need a square canvas that meets the FB ad dimensions. At the time I did this, those were 1080 x 1080.

So, File->New, Web, click on a preset and change it to 1080 x 1080. 72 DPI and RGB/8 should be fine.

Because you might use this more than once, let's create a preset with it. To do that, click on the + sign next to Custom at the top right side of the New Document dialogue box:

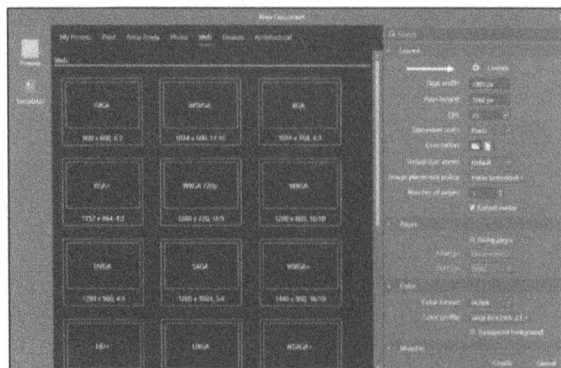

That will add a new preset to the My Presets section that is called Unnamed 1. (Your New Document dialogue box will move you over to that section automatically. The new preset is added at the bottom if you already had presets in there.)

Right-click on the Unnamed 1 thumbnail and choose Rename Preset from the dropdown menu. Type in the name you want for the preset and click OK.

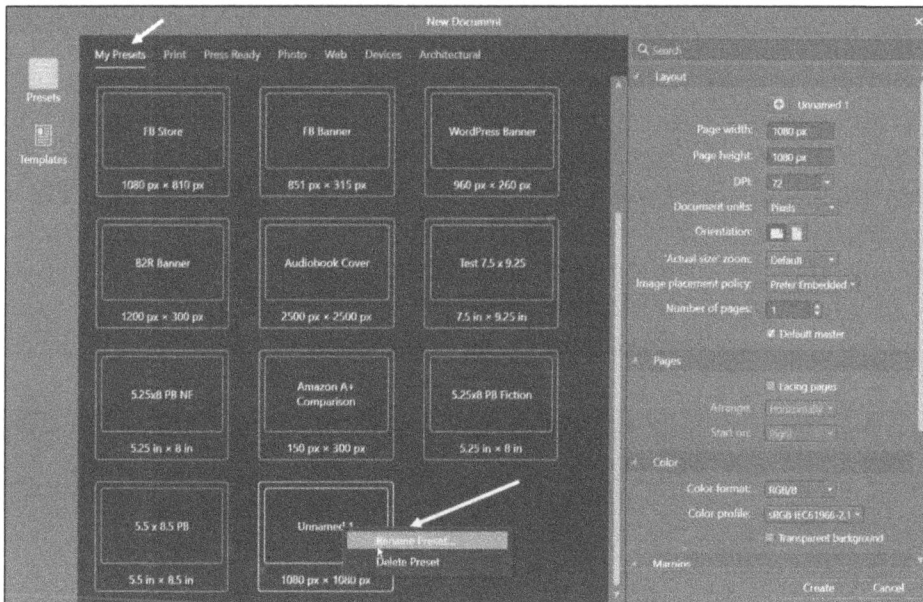

The preset will now show in your My Presets section with whatever name you gave it. For advertising and cover presets I tend to name them based on the place I'm advertising and the type of image it is. The dimensions show below the name, so I don't feel the need to add those in.

In this case I would use FB Square Ad for my name, for example.

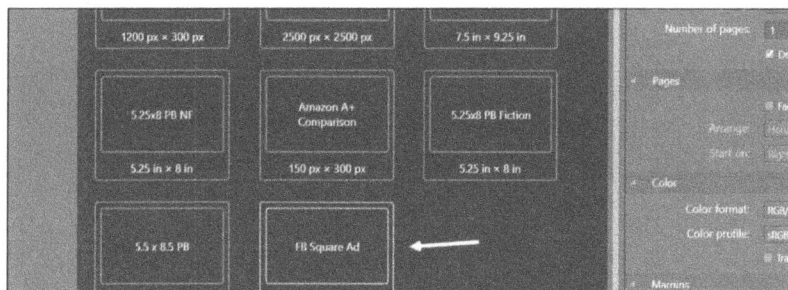

Once that's done and you've selected your preset, click on Create and you should have a nice white square canvas to work on.

* * *

Because I'm in the habit of working with picture frames, the first thing I do is insert a picture frame. So, click on the Picture Frame Rectangle Tool in the left-hand set of icons. (It's the rectangle with an X through it.) Left-click on one corner of your canvas, hold that down, and drag to the opposite corner of your canvas so that you have a picture frame that covers the entire square.

(You could just click and drag to cover the portion of the square where we're going to place the image, but I always draw it to cover the entire canvas. That way if I change my mind about the size or the location of the text element I don't have to also change the size of my picture frame.)

Once you have your picture frame, click on the Place Image Tool icon, navigate to where you have your image stored, and select it. Affinity should bring it into the workspace centered and resized for the size of the frame. Like so:

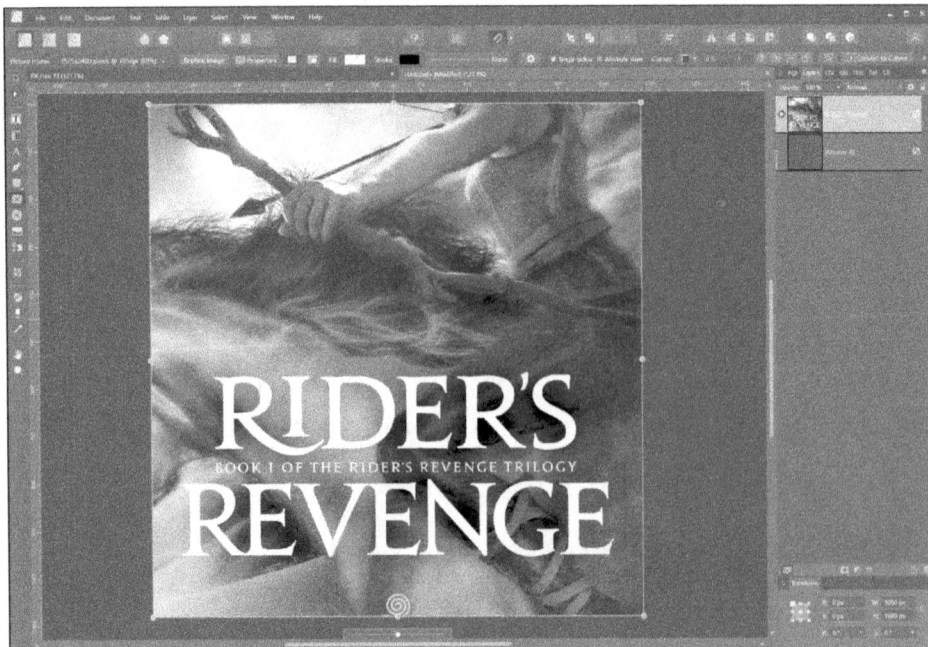

You can see I ended up with the text on the cover in my frame instead of the girl based upon where the center of the cover happened to fall.

I now need to reposition the image until I have the portion of the image I actually want in the picture frame. I can do this by clicking in the center of the arrows on the image in the workspace or by going to the image layer in the Layers studio and then repositioning the image that way.

When working in the image layer, if you click on the Move Tool first before you try to drag the image around it will make doing so easier.

If for some reason you have the text tool selected instead, you'll have to drag from one of the edges of the image to make it work.

(As an aside, when I find that I'm not able to click and move things the way I want or that I'm putting in extra layers I didn't intend to add, it usually boils down to an issue with which tool I have selected on the left-hand side. Usually I can fix a problem like that by clicking on either the Move Tool or the Artistic Text Tool.)

For this particular image, I not only had to drag it downward to focus on the girl on the horse, but I also had to make the image larger by using the slider under the image. I could have also clicked and dragged the image from the corner or used the Transform studio if I'd been in the image layer instead.

Remember that the tools available to you will depend on which layer you're clicked onto in the Layers studio.

Anyway. After a few rounds of moving and resizing the image, I ended up with this:

Much better.

Keep in mind with this that the entire cover imported. I didn't have to take the cover, trim out this part of the image, export that trimmed part to a JPG file, and then import it into my ad. The whole cover is still there. Which means if I decide this is off size-wise or position-wise, I can simply click and drag the image to fix it.

Alright, now it's time to add the text at the bottom.

The first thing I want is the black rectangle that will go in the background. To insert that I click on the Rectangle Tool (the blue filled-in box on the left-hand side set of icons) and then left-click and drag in the workspace to form the shape I want.

Mine inserted as white by default. Here it is:

If you look at the top of your workspace you should see a Fill option with a rounded rectangle next to it that is the same color as the rectangle we just inserted. (The Fill option will always be a rounded rectangle no matter what shape you actually insert.) I have an arrow pointing to it in the image above.

Click on that rectangle. Choose the Swatches tab. Click on the black square swatch at the far left end. This will turn the inserted rectangle black.

(If you didn't want black, this is where you'd choose pretty much any color you want, but for now we're going with black.)

Next I want to insert my text. I could just insert the text directly onto the black rectangle, but I want to put it in a text frame so that I can adjust the width and height of the space I'm centering my text within.

To insert a text frame, I go to the left-hand set of icons and click on the Frame Text Tool, which is the third one down and has a black capital T in a gray box.

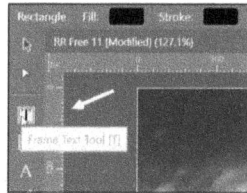

Once I've chosen the Frame Text Tool, I left-click and drag inside the perimeter of the black rectangle I just created to form a smaller rectangle. It shows as a blue border as I create it. Like so:

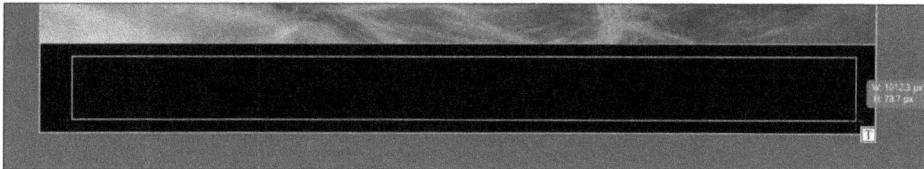

It doesn't have to be perfect. You can always click on it and drag the edges to adjust it later.

I do want to make sure that the frame is centered in my workspace, though. To do that I go to the Adjustment option up top (the one we used before that looks like a line with two blue bars coming off of the right side) and choose the Align Center option under Align Horizontally.

Now it's time to add my text to the text frame. To do that I click on the Artistic Text Tool on the left-hand side, which is a capital A.

Before I start typing, though, I go to the top of the workspace and click on the black rounded rectangle to change the font color to white. (Otherwise I'll start typing and won't see the text because it will be black on black.)

Remember, the most reliable way to change the color to white is to choose the Swatches tab and then choose the far right swatch which is the white one.

There is no label for that rounded rectangle, but it should be the only one you can see when the text tool is active. It's right next to the U for underline.

Once you've done that, click into the text frame and type your text. For this ad I am using "Download For FREE Today". Initially the text is going to be small and tucked away in the top left corner of the frame, like this:

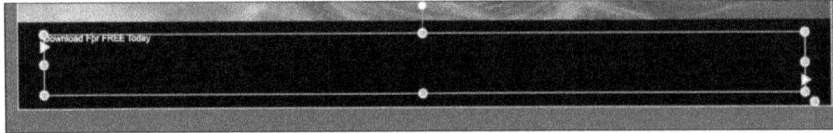

After you've typed in your text (which you can also see in the Layers studio, at least partially), use Ctrl + A to select all of it or highlight it with your mouse.

Next go to the top menu and change the font and font size. I'm using a font called Fontin SmallCaps which is available free for personal and commercial use.

Changing font and font size work just like they do in a standard word processing program. You can click on the arrow next to the current font name or size to see a range of available choices. Either click on the one you want or start typing in the box if you know what you already want.

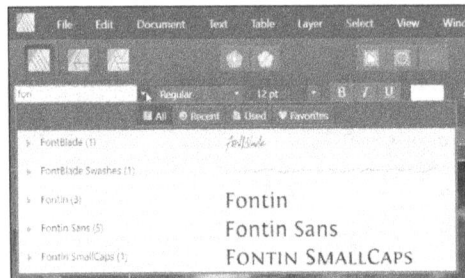

Here I started to type Fontin until I had a shortened list with that font in it and then I clicked on my selection.

If you're not sure what you want to use, you can always hold your mouse over an option to see what it will look like in your document. It will only be applied when you click on it.

I usually change the font first before I change the font size, because some fonts are very different from one another in terms of absolute size at a given point size.

For now I set my font to 72 point because 96 point took it past staying on one line. (If that happens the border around the text will show a red arrow on the right-hand side, indicating that there is additional text that is not currently visible.)

We'll probably come back to this in a minute and customize the point size, but it's a start for now.

Also, while we're still clicked into the text in the text frame we can center our text. Because it is in a text frame, it will center within the frame not within the overall document. This one we have to center differently than the others we've centered because we're centering text not a design element in the layout.

You should be able to see a series of text alignment options on the right-hand side of the dynamic menu above the workspace which is where you already changed the font and font size.

Each alignment option shows a series of lines that form a paragraph. The lines are arranged to show whether it's left-aligned, centered, right-aligned, or justified. You can also hold your mouse over each one to see what it is.

The second option there is to center text. Click on it.

If somehow you clicked away from where you were entering text, it's possible that when you go back to click on that text that Affinity will think you're trying to add a new line of text into your document and will insert a new layer for that.

If that happens (because I do this often), Ctrl + Z to undo the new layer you didn't want, then go to the Layers studio and click on the layer with the text that you wanted to edit first before you click in your workspace where that text is.

Okay, so here we are so far:

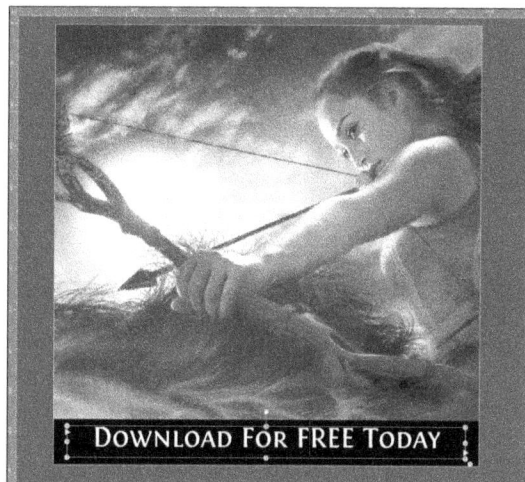

I want that text to also be aligned vertically within the text frame. Meaning I want as much space above it as below it in the text frame. (Right now it's top-aligned and you can see more space below the text in the text frame than above it. This is different from the amount of space in the black rectangle behind the text frame. We'll deal with that in a minute.)

To center text vertically within a text frame, use the dropdown option to the right of the horizontal alignment choices we just used. It's going to be the second dropdown option and you want to choose Center Vertically from that dropdown menu.

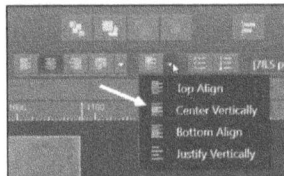

That will center the text within the text frame. (But not within the rectangle. We'll come back to that in a minute.)

Now it's time to place the three-dimensional book cover.

Once more I like to work with a picture frame. So I go to the Picture Frame Rectangle Tool on the left-hand side of my workspace, click on it, and then left-click and drag in my document to form a rectangle to place my cover within.

When I did this, the layer I created inserted in the Layers studio below my existing layer that had my background image. Which meant that if I went ahead and inserted my cover into the picture frame it wouldn't be visible on my canvas because the picture frame layer was completely covered by my background image.

So let's detour for a second and talk about layers and how they work with one another.

Here is my Layers studio right now:

You can see that the top layer has my cover image with the girl on the horse and my text. That is what will be visible in my document no matter what.

The only way to not have that top layer visible would be to reduce the opacity to 0% or to uncheck the box on the right-hand side.

Everything below the top layer will only show if the top layer doesn't cover that portion of the canvas. Since my background image covers the entire space, that means right now nothing below it will show. I need any additional layers I add, like my book cover, to go above the background layer.

So when I add a layer like I just did and it's placed below my background layer, I need to go into the Layers studio and move that layer up. The way to move a layer is to left-click on it and hold that left-click as you drag it to where you want it.

A light blue line will show when you drag your layer to a new location. Release your left-click when that light blue line is where you want the layer to be. (You can see that light blue line in the image below.)

You can also move a layer from being a subset of another layer. For example, when I initially added my rectangle and text those layers both were added in as subsets to the picture frame layer. I don't actually want that necessarily, so what I can do is group the rectangle and text so they can be moved together and then click and drag them up above the background picture frame layer so that they're standalone.

That's what's happening here:

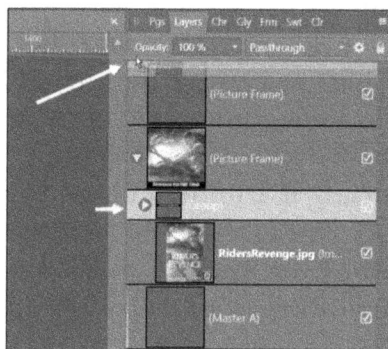

I have the Group layer that's the rectangle and text selected and I've dragged it to the top of my layers and am ready to release my left-click so that it's placed above my book cover picture frame and my background image picture frame.

I probably didn't have to group and move the text, it was visible from where it was, but I did it just to make sure that the text and its background would always be on top of all of the other layers. That way if, for example, my book cover stretched down into the space where I had my text it would do so behind the text, not on top of it.

Here's my new hierarchy:

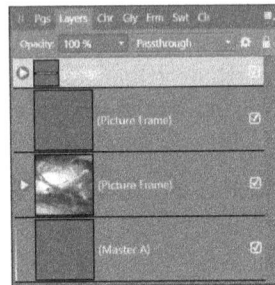

My text and black rectangle are in a group on top. Below that is my layer for my cover (that I have yet to insert), and below that is my background image. At the very bottom is the Master.

Always check your layer order to make sure that what needs to be on top is. If you swear you added an element and it isn't showing on your final then chances are the layer is too low in the hierarchy so some other element is hiding it or you unchecked the layer and forget to recheck it before you generated your final image.

Okay. I'm going to bring in that book cover now. To do so, I click on the Picture Frame layer for the book cover, then go to the Place Image Tool icon on the left-hand side, click on that, and then I find my 3D cover image and select it.

Affinity should insert the image into the frame at an approximate size that works for the frame, but usually you're going to need to adjust things a bit unless the cover image you're inserting is trimmed down to just the cover which these 3D templates tend not to do. Remember to click down to the actual image layer before trying to move or adjust the image if you do it that way.

(As a side note here, something I've touched upon before is that objects move differently depending on whether you have the Artistic Text Tool or the Move Tool selected on the left-hand side. Generally you can move an object with either one selected, but if you put your mouse over your workspace and see an A next to the cursor then the way to move the object is going to be to left-click on the outer border when you see a black four-sided arrow. Only then will you be able to move the image. If the Move Tool is selected, on the other hand, then you can left-click anywhere on the object to move it. This is something that will occasionally trip me up, so if you're having trouble moving something around, click on the Move Tool black arrow and try again. And, yes, I've said this more than once because it trips me up that often.)

Alright then. Here we are. We have one last thing to do and then we can optimize things.

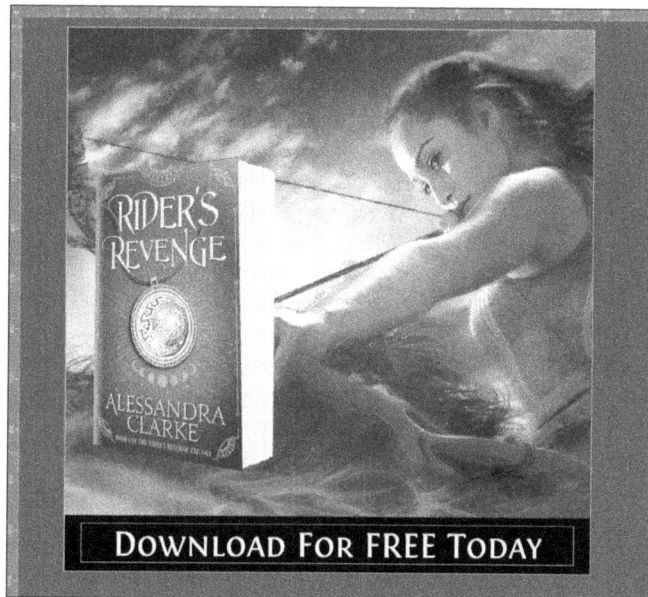

We need to turn the word FREE yellow. To do so, click on the A for the Artistic Text Tool on the left-hand side and then select the word FREE in your workspace. (Just left-click and drag to highlight.)

There are a couple of ways to change the color of your text. The first is to go to the white colored text rectangle up top in the dynamic toolbar and click on it to bring up the Swatches, Color, and Gradient options.

We already talked about how to use the Swatches option for white, black, and shades of gray as well as recent colors. (Just click over and click on the square for the color you want.)

When it comes to other colors, if you don't need an exact color you can click on the rainbow-shaded color bar at the top of the Hue option to choose a base color and then click anywhere within the rectangle of color below that to choose a specific color. Like so:

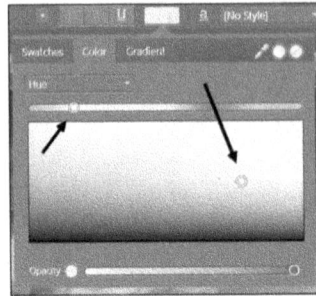

That often works for a generic color in a design, especially when working on a screen-based image where you don't have to worry about how it will print. But I find bright yellow a tricky one to get right, so I actually use a specific color for my bright yellow every time.

Which takes us to a different way to apply color.

Instead of clicking on the colored rectangle up top, I go to the Color studio in the top right corner. There I double-click on the circle that shows my current text color. In the screenshot it's a horrid sort of yellow, but yours is probably still white.

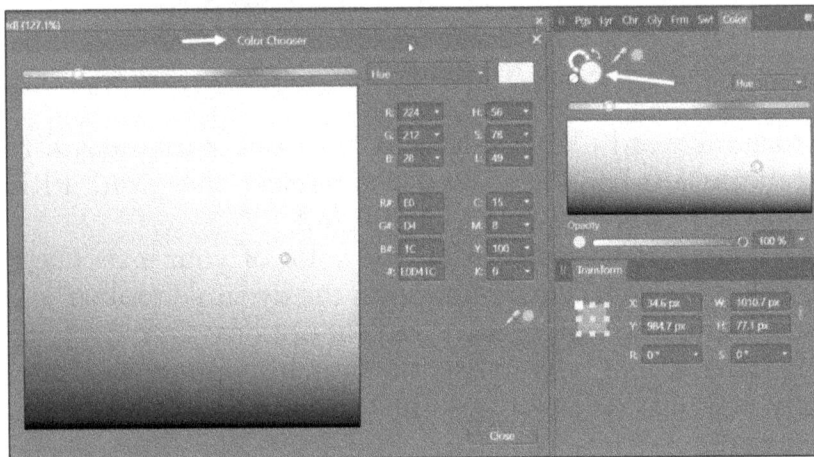

This will bring up the Color Chooser dialogue box where you can input your values for RGB, CMYK, HSL, or the Hex value for the specific color you want. The Hex value for the yellow I like is FFD500, so I type that in the box next to the # sign.

I could also type 255, 213, and 0 in the RGB fields, respectively, to get the same result. That changes the color of yellow for the selected text to the one I like to use.

You may not like that yellow. If you don't, then feel free to experiment around with the color mix for RGB or do a web search to find a specific color code.

Once that's done, this is what we have:

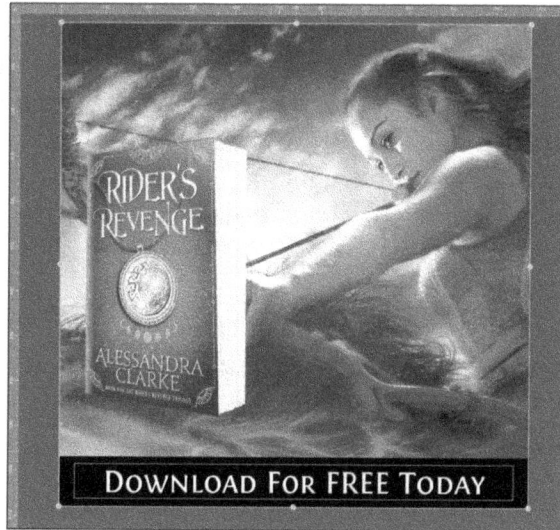

But…

The ad we were trying to replicate is more eye-catching.

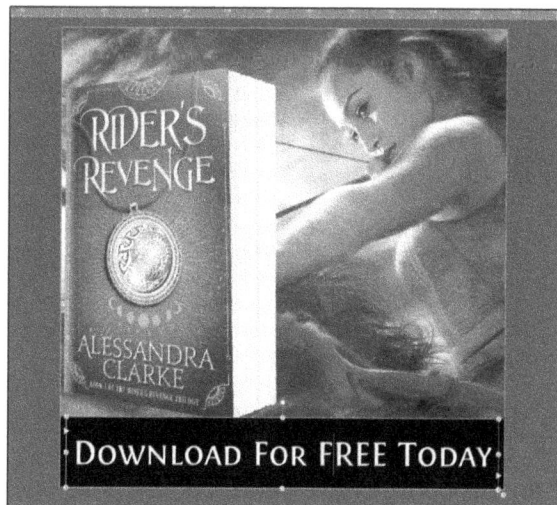

The cover was bigger. The background image was closer-up. The text was bigger.

We have the components in the right place, but they don't look as good as they could.

This is why it's always good to experiment with your ad images. Even if you know the components you want to use try variations where you change the size of the elements, change their position, change their colors, etc.

It's fiddly work, but it can make a big difference and as a more novice designer you probably don't yet have the instincts to get the optimal appearance the first time around. I certainly don't. As you can see above.

Now, let me show you a couple tricks.

First, if you ever do want to change the size of a picture frame, like I need to for the book cover component of this ad, you can also resize what's in the frame along with it and save a step.

To do so, click on the Move Tool and then click onto the book cover in the main document. Look for a blue circle *outside of* the main picture frame in the bottom corner. Click and drag on that circle to resize your frame and it will also resize the image at the same time.

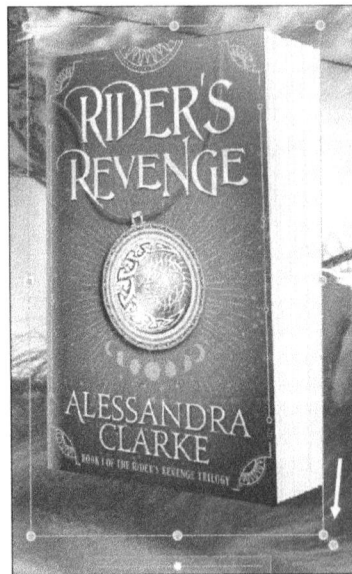

Second, don't forget that you can use the slider under the picture frame to change the size of just the image.

And you can click in the center of the four arrows in the center of the image to move just the image around.

Third, while you can also resize text frames and text together, you need to be careful doing so. It can skew your text in weird ways because it will stretch the text to fit. So if you change the height more than the width that will happen to the text, too. And sometimes the only way to fix it is to delete the text and retype it. (At least as far as I know.)

Okay. On this one, I'm going to resize the black rectangle, expand the text frame, and then bump up the font size for the text. I'm also going to change the background image size and reposition it. And change the book cover size and reposition that.

And here we go.

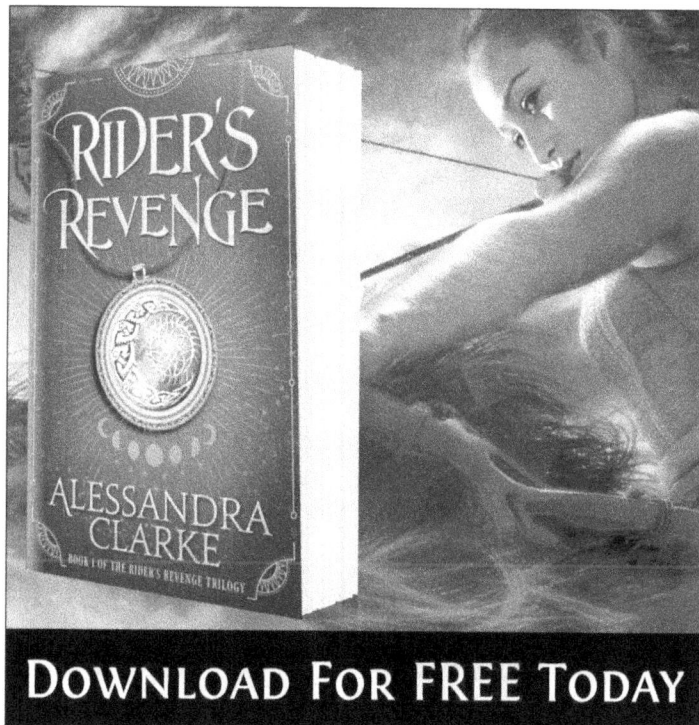

Better. Close to the original we were aiming for and much better than we originally ended with.

Or not

Because one of the nice things you can do with FB ads is have multiple ones running at once. For me aesthetically this ad looks better than the one where everything was smaller, but it's possible that the other image is the better one for selling this book.

And with FB I can run both ads and see which FB prefers and which gets me a lower cost per click and downloads per click.

Now, that probably seemed like a lot of effort for a simple ad. But that's because you're new to doing this. Once you get used to working in Affinity it can take maybe five or ten minutes to put something like that together.

Even better, you can always leverage what you've already done to make it even quicker.

We now have a square ad with download for free today at the bottom, a book cover on the left, and a cover image on the right. I can take that and have a new ad in less than five minutes.

Just to prove that to you I'm going to change this into an ad for book three of the series instead.

First step, I go to Document->Resource Manager and click on each row shown, choose Replace, find a replacement image for it, and select it.

That took maybe a minute to do and this is what I ended up with:

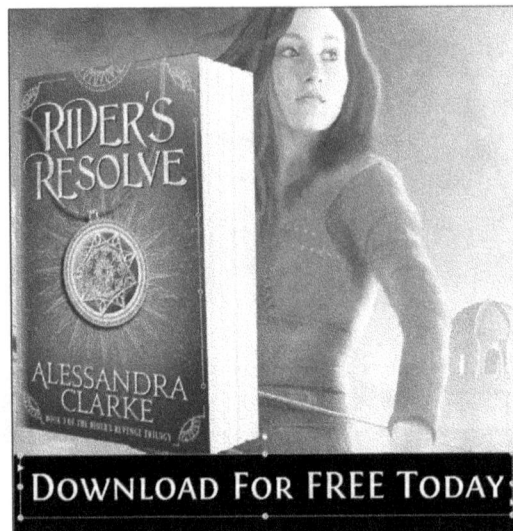

I still need to adjust the image in the background to create an ad that works better for this image, but it'll take me about two minutes.

Here we go:

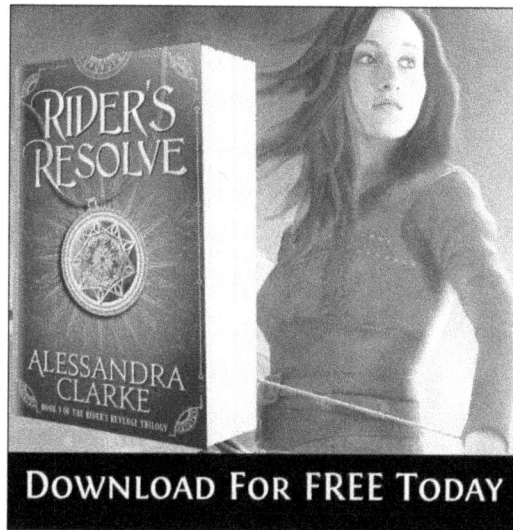

Fix the text that somehow got out of alignment and we're done in less than five minutes.

In this case, I swapped out both the cover and background image just to show you, but if I was only advertising that first book it takes even less time.

Obviously, the more different the original image and the new image are the more adjustment effort will be involved, but still, it's probably at most ten minutes to create a new ad once you have the components in place.

Definitely save a copy to use later.

Okay. That was FB ad number one. But you could argue that it worked because the covers are expensive covers. So let's do one now with a different layout that uses homemade covers instead. And a "homemade" image, too.

FACEBOOK SQUARE AD USING A SIDE IMAGE

This ad is going to show that you don't need expensive covers to have an effective ad. I ran this ad for my cozy series at the same exact time as I ran the ad above.

The cover is homemade, the book title probably sucks, and the ad image is a random photograph I took of my dog. Granted, she is photogenic, but still. Not ideal elements.

Here it is:

There's even a little bit of orange in the top of that image where I didn't size it correctly. But this ad generated clicks at a cost of 7 to 9 cents a click and resulted in downloads.

Why? Because it makes you stop if you like dogs. And it tells you that it's advertising a book. And that that book is free and has five star reviews from people who loved the dog. The text around the ad image tells you it's a mystery.

And that's really all that's needed. Free. Book. Dog Lovers. Mystery. (Assuming the book delivers on that promise, of course.)

Let's put this thing together. You obviously won't have my cute dog photo to work with, but substitute in your own or a cute kid photo or a hot guy or something that will appeal to your audience.

First things first, File->New, My Presets, FB Square Ad, Create. (Because you saved that as a preset, right? If not, go back to the last chapter for instructions on how to create your square ad to work with.)

Next, Rectangle Tool (the blue square), click and drag over the workspace. Change the color by clicking in the dynamic toolbar up top and using the Swatches tab to select the black square so that your canvas is now black.

After you've done that, click on the Frame Text Tool (the T in a frame) on the left-hand side and click and drag to draw a rectangle at the bottom of the workspace that will fit the review quote you've chosen.

Next, click on the Artistic Text Tool, change your color up top to white, click into the text frame you just created, and type in a dash followed by your review quote. In this case I'm using "I Loved Miss Fancypants!"

Select All (Ctrl + A), change the font and the font size using the dynamic menu up top. Be sure when you choose your font size that you leave enough room to add the five stars at the beginning.

Click back into the text you just added at the start of the text.

Go to the Glyph Browser studio, choose Wingdings from the top menu where the font is listed (remember that you can start typing in the font name to get to that part of the list), and scroll down in the main area of the studio until you see the star shape.

Double-click on it. It should insert into your document where you had your cursor and will also now be at the bottom of the glyph browser studio where your recently-used glyphs are displayed.

You can either go back to your main workspace and highlight and copy the star you inserted (Ctrl + C) and then paste it four more times (Ctrl + V), or you can stay in the Glyph Browser studio and double-click on the star glyph four more times.

Either way you should end up with five stars at the beginning of that line of text.

Readjust the font size or spacing of your text if you need to now that the stars are there, too.

Use the alignment options up top to center your text in the text frame vertically and horizontally. (They're the ones with lines in the dynamic menu in the second row up top that are located to the right of the middle. Vertical alignment is a dropdown menu.)

Once you've done that, you should have something that looks like this:

Now go to the Layers studio, right-click on the text layer, and choose Duplicate. This should create a second text layer directly on top of the first one.

Click onto that duplicate text layer in your workspace and drag upward until your duplicated layer is aligned with the top of the workspace. (Chances are you still have the Artistic Text Tool selected so remember that you can only click and drag from the edge of the layer. Either that or you need to switch over to the Move Tool before you try to move the layer. Also, snapping will let you know when you've dragged your duplicated text layer to the top.)

Next, make sure the Artistic Text Tool is selected and click into the text layer you moved. Delete the stars and the dash. Then delete the rest of the text and replace it with "Download For FREE Today".

(If you delete all of the text at once you'll default to the Wingdings font when you add new text and instead of typing the letter D you'll be typing in a mailbox instead. Which you can do if you want to. Just select all and change the font after you're done.)

Once the new text is added, Select All with Ctrl + A, and change the font size so that the text fills the space as much as possible. Your text should still be centered within its text frame, but if it isn't, fix that, too.

You should now have something like this:

Next step is to color the word FREE and the five stars yellow. Select the word FREE, click on the Color studio tab, double-click the circle for your main color which will likely be white, and type in FFD500 for the color value in the # field (or whatever color value you want to use).

For the five stars you can select them and then either do that again or go to the Swatches studio and click on the yellow-colored swatch from the Recent section. (You can also access Swatches from the colored rectangle in the dynamic menu at the top.)

After you've changed the color of the stars and the word FREE, it's time to add your images.

Click on the Picture Frame Rectangle Tool (looks like a rectangle with an X on it) in the left-hand side set of icons, and then click and drag to draw a rectangle in your workspace that stretches between the two text frames and is 360 pixels wide. (Using the rule of thirds, we divide 1080 by three to get 360.)

As you align the picture frame with the edges of the text frames and of the master you should see the red and green snapping lines to tell you've aligned with the edges

Next, place your three-dimensional cover in the picture frame by clicking on the Place Image Tool (landscape image on the left-hand side) and selecting your cover from where you have it saved.

Once the cover has been inserted, adjust the image so that it's fully visible and centered in the frame.

You should now have something like this:

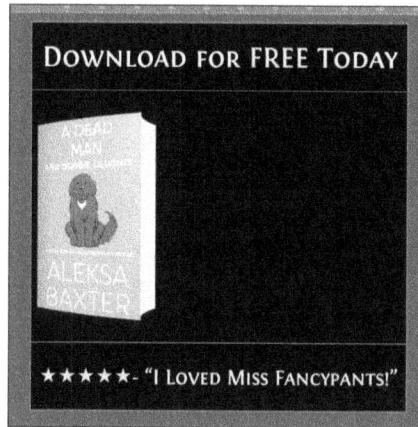

Add another picture frame that covers the remaining area. I actually made mine 693 not 720 because I thought 720 would crowd the book cover too much.

Insert your chosen image and adjust to fit the frame.

In my case, the picture came in sideways, so let's discuss how you can fix that.

Option one is to click and drag on the white circle at the top of the perimeter of the image. As you hold your left-click and drag, the image should rotate with your mouse.

Here you can see the image in mid-rotation. I have an arrow pointing at the white circle:

Another option is to change the R value in the Transform studio. In this case a -90 degrees worked to change the orientation.

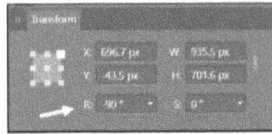

If you use the Transform option, it may move the image to a location outside of the picture frame, and you'll have to drag it back into frame.

As you work to position your image, Affinity should provide green or red alignment lines for the alignment of the image within the picture frame. Here, for example, the image is centered in the frame so there is a green line showing down the center of the picture frame:

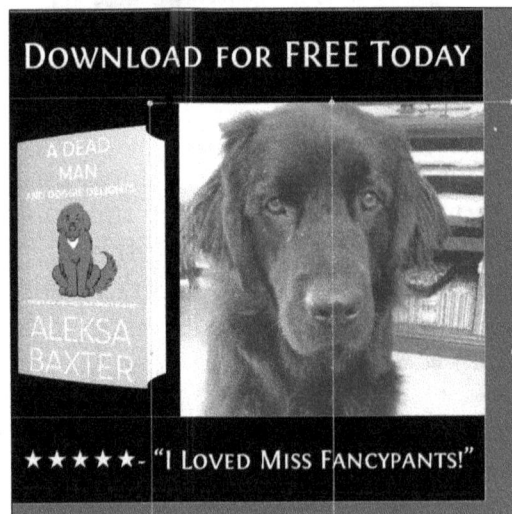

The problem with relying on these lines is that Affinity is using the entire image, and the center of the image may not actually be the center of the part of the image that you want to emphasize.

For example, here the dog is off-center of the frame even though the overall picture is centered. I don't want that much of the background bookcase to show on the right-hand side of the picture frame so I need to adjust manually instead.

When I do that, here is our final version:

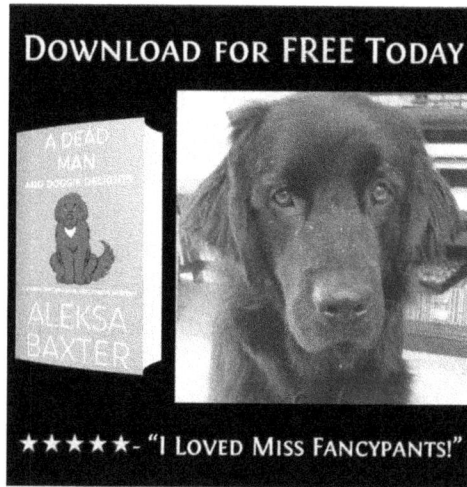

(And I can attest that even though it's slightly off from the original, it still works just fine because I uploaded it to FB after I created it and it gave me 6 cent clicks the first day.)

* * *

Very basic, right? But it gets the point across. Do you love dogs? Then look, free. Book. Five stars.

The other ad that ran at the same time and did just as well was this one:

It does the exact same thing. Look, dog. Free. Book. Five stars. And because these are cozies, bright colors work.

Again, once you create one of these it's a very simple matter to swap out a book or an image or a quote to get a new ad image.

* * *

One more thought about these two ads we just did.

I personally prefer to put my text on a solid background because it's easier for someone viewing the ad to see what the text says. But I've seen successful ads that didn't set the text apart like that.

Although the ones that put text on a textured background still tend to mute the background enough that the text is the main component of that part of the image.

The key is to experiment and see what works for your books and your audience.

* * *

Okay. So far what we've done has been very basic. We haven't manipulated any images at all, we've just brought them into Affinity. We've basically been building with pre-formatted puzzle pieces.

But now let's experiment a bit and bring in images that we manipulate. To shake things up, I'm going to do this one as a BookBub CPC ad but what we're going to do will work for any ad image you want to create. The key is to keep in mind proportion and balance for each ad size.

BOOKBUB AD WITH IMAGE ADJUSTMENTS AND 99 CENT LABEL

Originally I was going to use another FB ad for this chapter, but I just looked at a few of my old ad images and decided they weren't very good so I didn't want to use them. And that's something you're going to have to accept as you learn to do your own ads. Sometimes you think you did a good job with something, but you really didn't. And worse, sometimes you don't realize it until you look back later. So there you were, out in public, looking bad.

But this entire industry—including the writing—is about taking your hits, learning from them, and improving for the next go round.

So I'm going to do something risky here and we're just going to build an ad from scratch. Which means that three months from now I might flip through this book and think, "Wow, that was an ugly ad image, why on earth did I use that in that book?"

It happens. But no matter how bad the ad we're about to create turns out, at least you'll learn the additional skills I wanted to show you and you can do a better job with your own ads.

Here goes.

According to their FAQs BookBub CPC ads need to be 300 x 250 pixels. So File->New, Web, 300 width, 250 height, 72 DPI is fine, landscape orientation, RGB/8. Feel free to turn this into a preset that you save in your My Presets section for future use. If not, just click Create.

You should now have a big white almost-square rectangle to work with.

I'm going to use my fantasy cover for this one (because it's more forgiving) and I actually want to use the colors from the cover in the rest of my ad, so the first thing I'm going to do is bring in the cover.

Picture Frame Rectangle Tool. Add the cover with the Place Image Tool. Adjust to fit.

Here we go with a picture frame that is 150 W by 235 H:

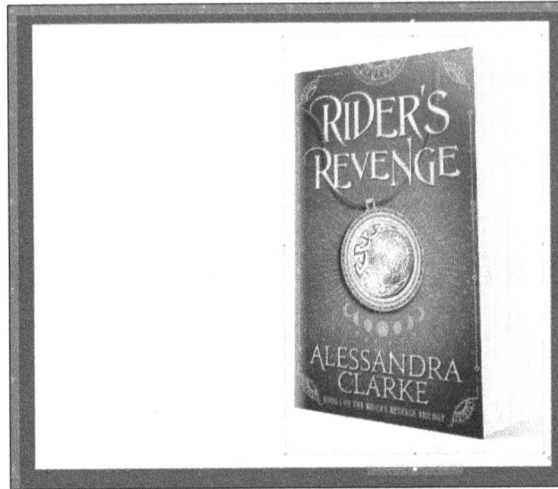

Now, the reason I brought in the cover first is because I don't want to use black this time. I want to tie into the colors in that cover. So my next step is going to be to add a rectangular space at the bottom (using the Rectangle Tool) and to color that rectangle a color that corresponds to the cover.

First things first, I move the cover up a bit and then use the Rectangle Tool to click and drag my rectangle into place at the bottom.

To use the color from the cover, I go to the Color studio and left-click on the eyedropper and then hold down that click as I move my mouse over my cover. You can see the circle that surrounds my mouse as I do this.

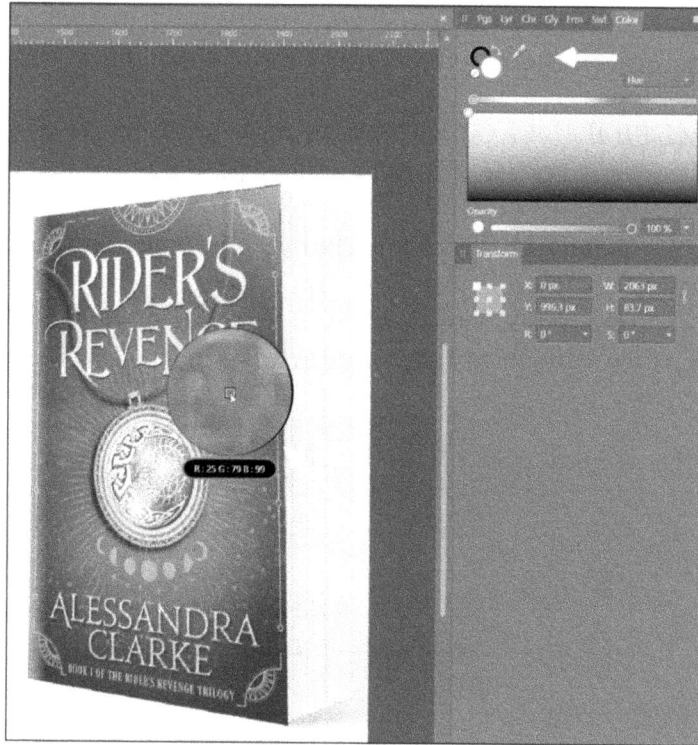

Also, the color in the circle next to the eyedropper up in the Color studio will change to reflect my currently selected color.

Once I have a color I like, I can just let up on the left-click to choose it. (You can see that the color on this cover is not uniformly one color so I have a range of options to choose from. With some of my other covers where I used a solid fill for the background I'd just have one single option.)

That chose the color for me, but to actually use it I need to double-click on the colored circle next to the eyedropper in the Color studio. That will make it my main color and also should apply it to my rectangle at the same time.

(The only reason it wouldn't is if you had the border option instead of the main color option selected for some reason. Remember the main color is the solid circle, the border color is the doughnut and whichever is on top is the one you're working with in the Color studio.)

Once you select the color it will also be available in your Swatches studio under Recent in case you need it again.

Okay. Next I want to add text to my rectangle. In this case I'm going to use some bulleted descriptions separated by a moon glyph which fits the theme of the cover and the book.

I'm not going to put this one into a text frame, so I just click onto the A for the Artistic Text Tool on the left-hand side of the workspace and then click onto my ad and start to type.

My text is "MEDDLING GODS HIDDEN CONSPIRACIES ENEMIES AS ALLIES." I'm going to use a font on this called Desire because that will go well with the cover text.

I use Ctrl + A to select all and then change the font and font size up top in the font dropdowns.

I also want to change the color of my text, so next I click on the black rectangle for the color option in that same row.

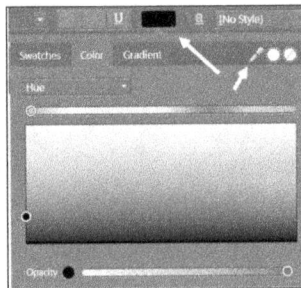

And once more I'm going to use a color from the cover. So I left-click on the eyedropper and hold that left-click until I take the color for my text from the cover. To apply it to my text, I double-click on the circle next to the eyedropper once it has a color showing.

Now it's time to add the moon symbols that I'm going to use between the descriptive phrases.

First step, I click back into my text after the word GODS, add a space, and then go to the Glyph Browser studio.

I want the Wingdings 2 font and then the quarter moon symbol that's after the numbers but before the clocks. I double-click to insert into my text. I do the same after the word CONSPIRACIES.

Be sure to add the extra space *before* you add the symbol because if you add the space after you add the symbol it may be a different sized space and that will make your text look uneven. (Ask me how I know. Ctrl + Z, Undo, is my best friend.)

At this point I adjust the font size again if I need to. I prefer to select all and manually change the font size in the dynamic menu at the top, but you can also click and drag on the box around the text to resize everything that way. Just be careful, because sometimes it will stretch out the text in weird ways if you do that.

To center the text element in your workspace, click on that layer in the Layers studio, and then use the Alignment option in the top row (the one with the line and two blue bars) and choose Align Center from the Align Horizontally section.

Here's what I get after that's all done:

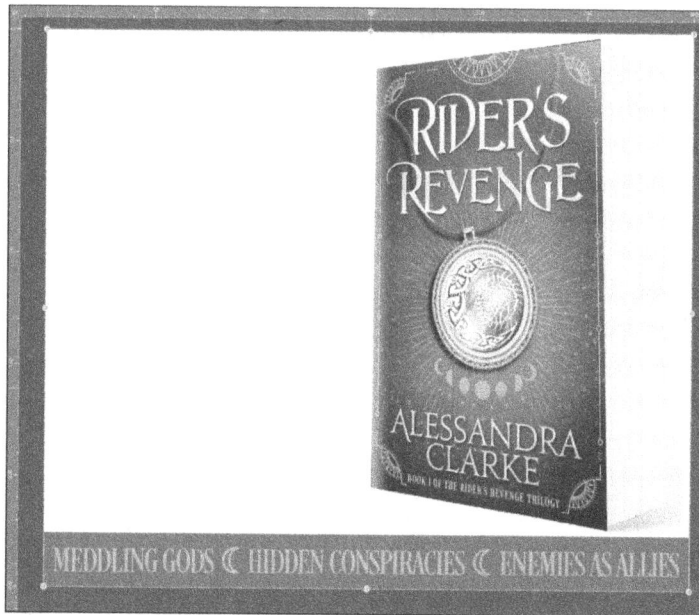

I'm not sure that text at the bottom is bright enough. I took it from the full moon on the cover, but I think I want to change that out for the brighter color in the author name. So let me do that now. I go back and select all the text by clicking on my text layer in the Layers studio, making sure my A is clicked on in the left-hand set of icons, and then clicking into my text.

Ctrl + A to select all.

Next I click on the text color in the dynamic menu up top, click on the eyedropper and hold as I select my new color, and then double-click on that circle next to the eyedropper to apply it.

Better.

(And if I didn't like it and decided the first color was better I have the option to Undo. Or I can go to the Swatches panel and click on the old color from there because it was used in the document so should be available to select there until I close the file. And if neither one is right, I can try again to get a color from the cover that I think works better. Or start clicking around for nearby color options in one of the color dropdowns.)

Okay.

Time to bring in an image for the background. I could use my original cover, but I'm going to actually use a stock photo for this. And we'll do this one without a picture frame for now, too, just so you can see how that works.

So, go to the Layers studio, click on the Master A layer, then click on the Place Image Tool, and find the image you want. Select it and then click and drag to insert.

Here we go.

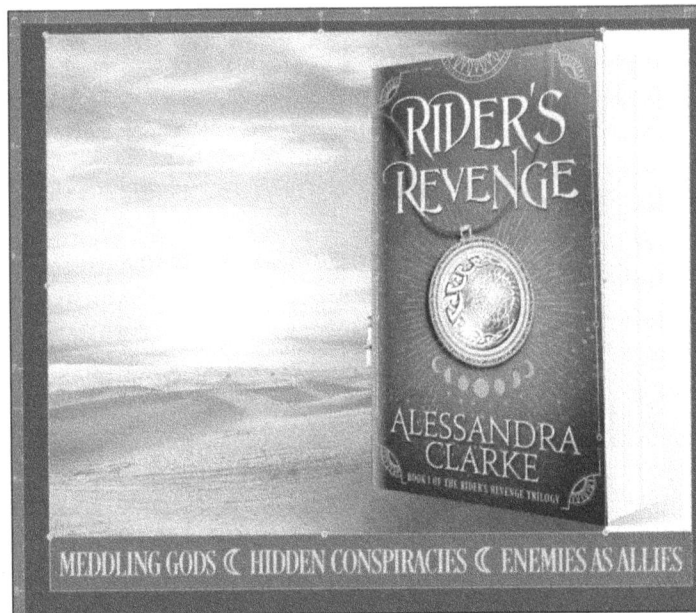

This was an image of a desert city, but the city is currently hidden behind the cover.

And the image doesn't currently fit the entire space. I can click and drag the image to make it bigger, but I don't want to. I want that city to be near to the size it is now. It needs to attract attention, but not too much attention.

Which means I need to find a way to fill that extra white space that the image doesn't cover. But before we deal with that, I want to flip my image so we can see the city on the left-hand side of the ad.

I do that by going to Layer->Transform->Flip Horizontal.

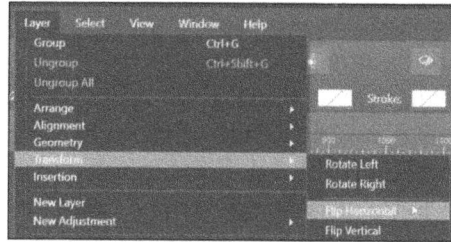

If you ever flip an image like this—and I find it can be handy to do at times—the next thing you need to do is make sure that the image still works. Was there any text in the image that is now backwards or upside down? (If you flip vertically.) Does the perspective look skewed now? Does it just seem off?

Also, if you flip an image like I just did here and then use the resource manager to replace the image, the new image will also be flipped. And any transformations you applied to the image will also be applied to the new one.

This has messed me up a few times, so it's worth mentioning. If you're going to do a lot of image manipulation on one image but not others for an ad, you might want to save a clean version of your file first before you start that manipulation work. (You can at least turn off a lot of effects in the Layers studio, though, if you don't do that.)

Anyway. My image is now flipped, but it's still not covering the whole space.

I can fix some of that with resizing.

Because I am not working in a picture frame, if I resize the image beyond the borders of my ad the image will be fully visible in my workspace even though it won't appear in the final ad I create. Like you can see here where my Pages studio shows what the ad would actually look like but the workspace shows the full image going beyond the boundaries of my canvas:

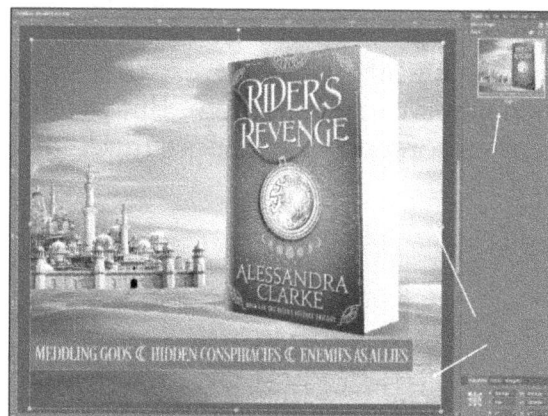

The background image you can see above has gone beyond the perimeter of the ad on the right-hand side as well as the bottom.

I personally find it a challenge to work with an image like this because it makes it harder to properly balance my different elements when what I can see on the screen is not what will appear in the ad. This is why I usually use picture frames.

And if I were going to keep this image at the larger size I have it at right now, I'd probably add a picture frame and drag the image into the frame to eliminate that issue.

But we're going to do something different here. We're going to duplicate this image layer, flip it back to the original orientation, and then line the edges of the two images up. Since the merge line will be hidden behind the cover this is a quick and dirty way for us to fill in that last little bit of white space in a way that matches the rest of the image.

It's not something I'd recommend where details really matter (like in the center of a cover), but for something like this that's going to be in the background behind another element it should work.

First step, click on the image layer in the Layers studio, right-click, Duplicate. Next, Layer->Transform->Flip Horizontal. Finally, click and drag on the new layer until you see the green line that shows the old and new layer are touching but not overlapping.

You also want the red lines at top and bottom to show they're aligned that way as well.

A way to confirm that the images are aligned top to bottom is to click on each layer and look at the Y value in the Transform studio. They should be the same.

If I think I might change the size of the background layer or move it around more, then I can select both layers now and group them so that they will move together or resize together. (Click on one layer in the Layers studio, hold down Ctrl and click on the other, then Ctrl + G or right-click and choose Group from the dropdown to group them.)

A note here that if you had these two layers in a picture frame sometimes weird things can happen when you group them. But for this, they should be fine.

So where are we at the moment? If I export this right now, this is what we have.

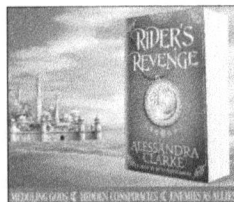

Which is fine. Not great. Not, wow I want that book right now, but it might be good enough to get clicks.

Let's try something to make it pop more. I'm going to put in lines to divide this space in thirds and see where they fall.

But first, the image falling outside of the workspace now that I've duplicated it is throwing my eye off, so I am going to go ahead and add a picture frame and drag the background image into it.

To add the picture frame, I go to Picture Frame Rectangle Tool, click and drag to add it and then move the edges of the frame until it aligns along the edges of my canvas. (Sometimes when you have elements already in your design it's easier to click further inside or even outside the edges of the canvas and create a frame and then drag the edges of the frame to the perimeter after that.)

Once I have my frame I go to the Layers studio, left-click on my grouped background images, and drag that group to the new picture frame layer.

Sometimes when you do this, the layer you dragged into the frame will disappear, so you have to be careful what part of the picture frame layer you drag onto. Try dragging to the left-hand side to get it to nest properly.

The background images should be added in as a subset of the picture frame. Like so:

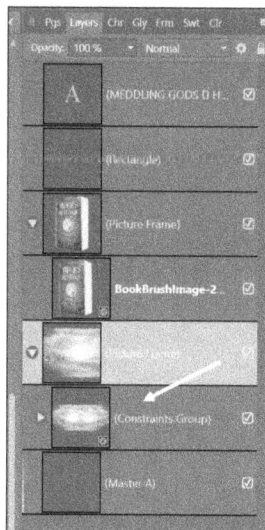

That's much easier to work with for me. Nice clean edges that don't go past the edge of my canvas.

Also, be sure that the picture frame layer for the background is the layer just above your Master A layer so that it truly is in the background. You don't want it to cover one of your other elements.

Okay. Now that we've cleaned things up, let's divide this space into thirds.

We have a width of 300, so that's going to be 100 and 200 where we need our guide lines. For the height we start with 250, but the rectangle I added is 24.3 so let's say 25, that gives me 225, divide by three and we get 75 so we need guide lines at 75 and 150.

The way to place a guide line is to left-click on the ruler on the side or the top of the black area in your workspace and then drag into your image.

As you drag you should see a light blue line and a small box that shows the X or Y location of your line. So in this picture it's a little hard to see but I've dragged my guide line 200 pixels into the document.

For a vertical line you drag from the side. For a horizontal line you drag from the top. If you need to adjust the placement of a line after the fact, left-click on it and drag. (You may need to click on the Move Tool first to be able to left-click on the line.)

Here is my document now with guide lines for the thirds.

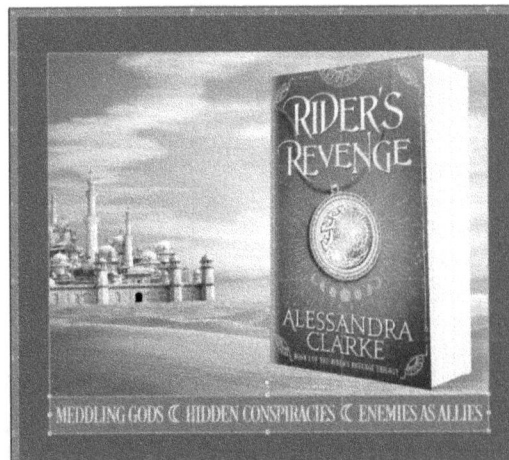

So what do we do with this?

Unfortunately these elements aren't in great spots. That power position in the top left third is empty sky. But the city does fit nicely in the second third on the left side. And our main element in the book cover is falling fairly nicely onto the right-hand third line and then in the center third section.

I could increase the size of the city to fall more into that power position, but then I move the emphasis from the book cover to the city and we don't want that. But I can move the image up a bit to align the line within the city to the second horizontal blue line we inserted.

And maybe I can bump up the background image size a bit. Now that we have the two images joined, it's a little harder to click and drag from a corner, so I'm going to click on the grouped image layer and use the Transform studio instead.

Before I change either the H or W values for the image in the Transform studio, though, I need to be sure to click on the two little circles with a line between them to the right of the W and H value fields to Lock Aspect Ratio.

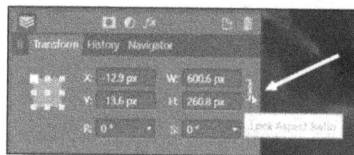

You lock the aspect ratio so that the width and height of the element adjust together. This keeps the image from becoming skewed. It doesn't matter with a solid background or a frame, but it matters very much with any image you work with.

And now we experiment resizing and adjusting our elements to get them to work the best together while keeping the emphasis on the book cover.

You can zoom in or out on your workspace using View->Zoom and then choosing from the options there. (Since this is a smaller image, zooming to 100% actually makes it pretty tiny.)

After some back and forth, here's where I ended up.

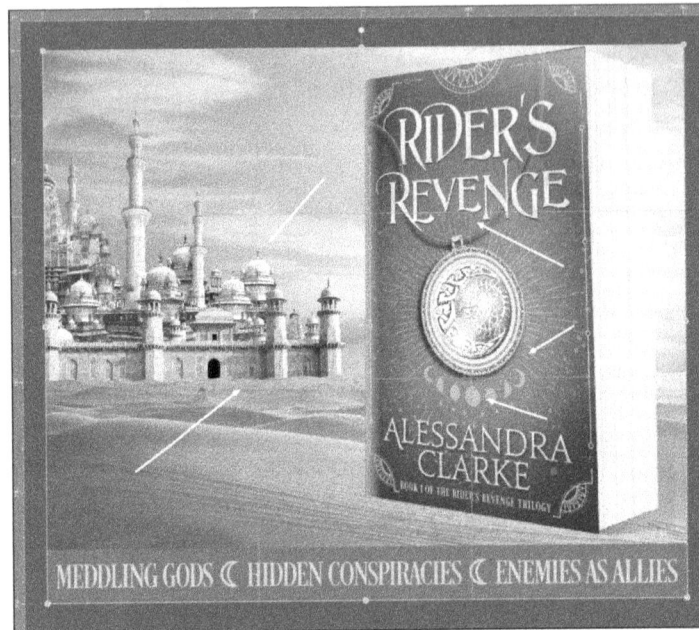

Note that the city is now sitting along the second horizontal line. And that the text of Revenge in the cover is sitting along the first. And that the central image in the cover is resting upon the second horizontal line and mostly at the intersection with the second vertical line. The E in Rider's is also now on the second vertical line.

Is it perfect? No. But I think at this point it would serve its purpose. The eye is drawn to the cover. The image in the background conveys the setting. The text along the bottom adds more information if people want it.

It's not the best ad ever. But it would probably generate clicks and sales.

Since we're here, though, let's talk about some other things you could do to that background image. (For those of you reading this in black and white what we're about to do may not look all that different and for that I apologize. You can do this on your screen as you read along to see what happens.)

Okay.

Go to the Layers studio and click on the background image under the picture frame and then go down to the bottom and click on the little icon that's a half-filled circled. If you hold your mouse over it, it's called Adjustments.

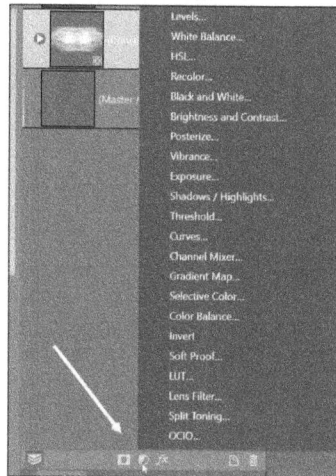

Right next to it is an *fx* icon that's called Layer Effects that will open a Layer Effects dialogue box for you.

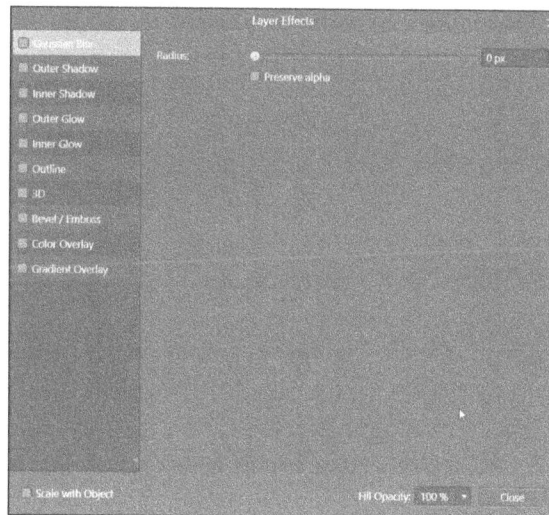

These are the two places where most of the adjustments you can make in Affinity Publisher are located. (Photo as I mentioned before has a lot more that you can do.) You can also access these through the Layer->New Adjustment and Layer->Layer Effects options in the top menu.

Most of these options we're not going to cover here, but feel free to experiment with them.

The one that I want to show you now is an effect that makes an image black and white.

Go to Layer->New Adjustment->Black and White up top or right-click on the Adjustments option I just showed you and then choose Black and White from the dropdown menu.

That will immediately turn the image black and white. It will also give you a Black and White dialogue box where you can adjust how different colors in the image are converted to black and white.

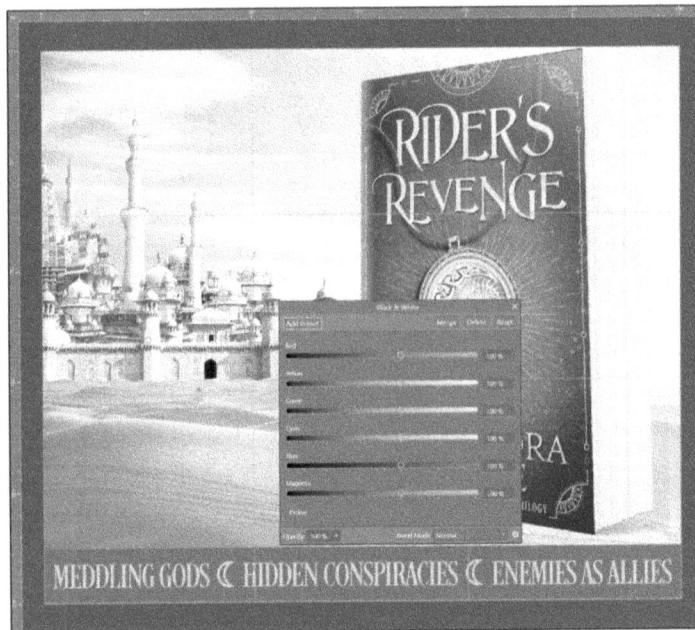

The image I'm using is mostly pinks and oranges, so adjusting the slider for blue doesn't really change anything, but using the red or magenta sliders definitely does.

That Blend Mode dropdown at the bottom can give you all sorts of interesting effects, but if what you want is just a basic black and white image, then keep it on Normal.

We can then add on top of that a Color Overlay to create a sepia-like appearance. First, make sure the layer is selected in your Layers studio and then open the Layer Effects dialogue box. (The little *fx* icon I mentioned above or go to Layer->Layer Effects to bring up the Layer Effects dialogue box.)

Click the checkbox for Color Overlay and then click on the words Color Overlay. That should turn the entire image black or whatever the color showing for color overlay is.

The Color Overlay settings should look like this:

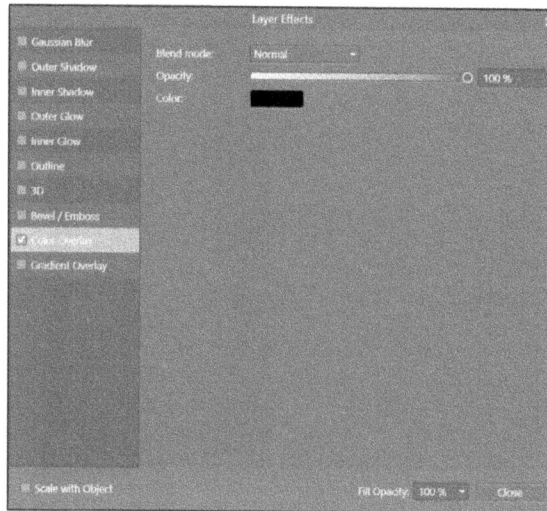

(The Layer Effects dialogue box can be weird sometimes because you can check a box for an effect but it doesn't actually take you to the settings for that effect when you do so, so be sure to click on the effect name to bring up the settings.)

To see the image under the overlay, you need to change the Opacity setting. You can either type in a value, or left-click on the circle and drag along the slider until you like what you see.

Before I do that, though, I'm going to click on the black rectangle next to Color, go to my Swatches option in the dropdown menu, and change the color. I'm going to try using the color that I pulled from the moon.

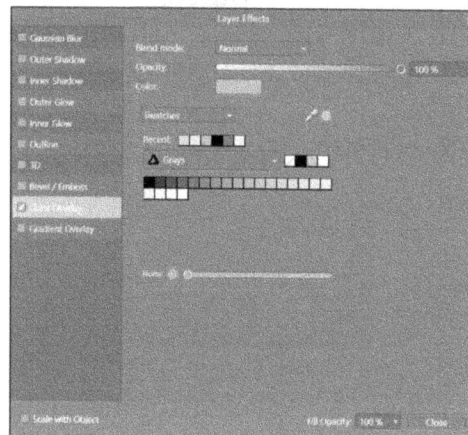

With my opacity at 45% here is my ad:

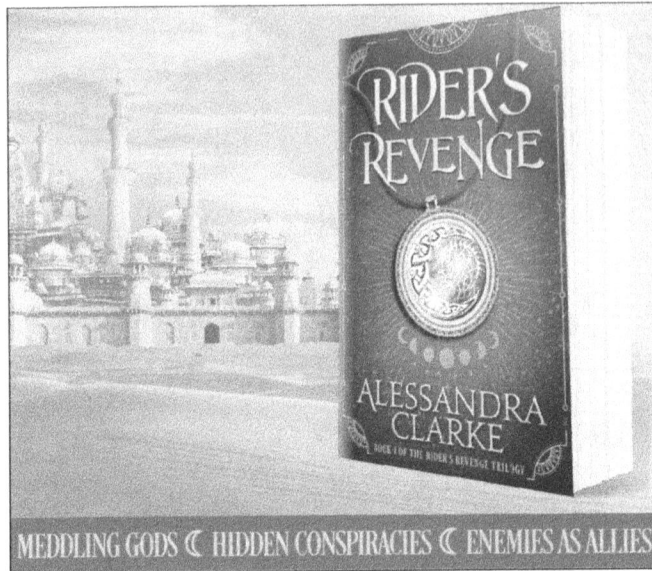

That bright pink and orange image is now a sort of muted beige in the background and the cover is definitely the focus.

Is that better than the colored version? Eh, I don't know. The color pulls the eye better, but maybe it muddies things up for a viewer and they don't know where to focus their attention.

But that's the beauty of CPC ads. You can put up a lot of variations and see which ones turn out to be the most clickable. (Just be sure you're also looking for sales or downloads, too. Clicks without purchases are just money spent.)

One more thing to mention on these effects. They are non-destructive, meaning you have not changed the underlying image. You can remove them easily by unchecking their box.

For the black and white adjustment, it's done in the Layers studio.

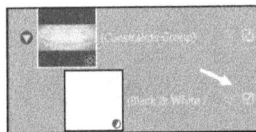

For the Color Overlay it's done by opening the Layer Effects dialogue box and unchecking the adjustment from there.

So don't be afraid to experiment with different adjustments. You can also delete the ones in the Layers studio. Just click on the white image portion of the layer to make sure you've selected that layer and then right-click, Delete from the dropdown.

One last thing we need to cover and that's how to add an element to your ad that says either "Free" or "99 Cents" or something like that.

The first thing we need is to click on the Rectangle Tool, but this time I'm going to click on the white arrow in the corner to see the full list of options, and I want to choose the Star Tool.

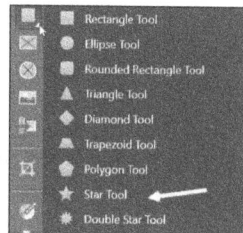

I can draw a star using the Star Tool just like I drew a rectangle with the Rectangle tool: left-click and drag on the canvas.

If you drag at an angle, it should stay proportionate. Here is my first attempt:

I think I actually want it more squat than that so I'm going to resize from the bottom a bit. To do so I just left-click and drag on that blue circle on the bottom border.

Next step is to click on the A for the Artistic Text Tool and type whatever it is you want, "Free", "99 Cents", etc. If you want to use the actual cents sign, use the Glyph Browser studio for that.

You can click on your text layer and then click and drag from the corner to resize the text to fit neatly into the star. Or you can always just change the font size in the dynamic menu up top until it fits well.

I like to position the text layer on top of the star so that it mostly fills the interior and is centered nicely. Here's what I ended up with:

My star background defaulted to the background I'd used for the rectangle at the bottom of the screen and the text color I'd used for the text I added down there. It blends well, but maybe I don't want it to blend. Maybe I want it to stand out strongly as the primary reason to click.

If that's the case then I should click on my star layer in the Layers studio, go to the Color studio, and change my color over to something like my bright yellow. Which then requires selecting the text and changing it to a different color as well, maybe a bright blue since that's the color on the opposite side of the color wheel from the yellow I'm using.

At this point, I go to the Layers studio, select the text and star layers, and group them so that they stay together and I don't have to reposition my text on my star if I move things around or resize them.

Now it's time to decide where you want your star and how big you want it to be.

I tend to prefer to put anything like this in touch with the cover, so I'm going to put it on my first horizontal dividing line, but not at that power point that's the intersection with the first vertical dividing line.

Also, I think I want the colored background instead of the muted one if I'm going to use a bright yellow star, so let me do that as well. And this is what I get.

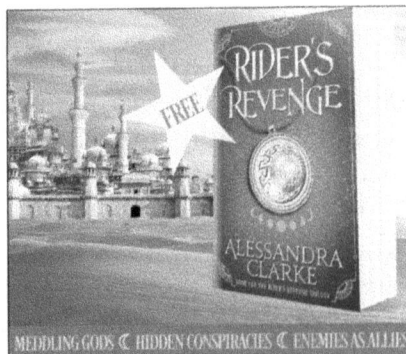

I'm not sure the star adds to the image, but I'd try it and see what the results were.

Looking at this now as I edit this book there are some more tweaks I would probably make. I'm not sure I like the moon symbols for my dividers and if I did keep the star with free on it I might try moving it around. But it probably works okay. And there's only so much time you can spend on something like this before you just have to give it a try and see if it gets you profitable sales.

EXPORT, SAVE, AND MORE

Before we wrap up, just a few more things you need to know.

EXPORT

To take the finished image you've designed and export it for upload to your chosen advertising platform, go to File->Export in the top menu.

This should bring up the Export Settings dialogue box.

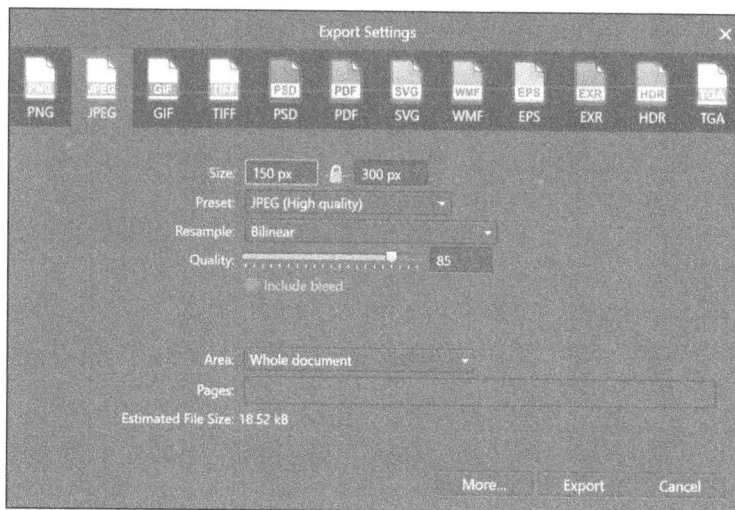

For the images we dealt with in this book you're going to want to click on the JPEG icon in the top row of choices.

I usually set my quality to 85% or so. (I used to set it 100% but setting it lower saves on file size and doesn't appear to have a strong impact on the image quality. I ran into a few sites that rejected my files as too big when the setting was at 100%.)

For Area you want the whole document and you don't need any special settings or to change the default preset.

Once you're ready, click Export. Choose your file location, verify the file name or assign a file name, and save.

Be certain that your file is exporting where you want it to. Mine defaults to wherever I exported to last and this sometimes gets me in trouble if I work on more than one project in a day. So always double-check before you export.

As you can see in that screenshot, there are a number of other file types you can choose for your export, but I believe JPEG should work for all advertising options.

I do use PNG when I have to export an image with a transparent background such as a three-dimensional cover. I leave all of the settings as is so it's just a matter of clicking on PNG up top in the dialogue box.

TIFF images are what you should use if you're creating a print interior.

PDF are required for print covers, but I cover that in *Affinity Publisher for Basic Book Covers*. If you need to export to PDF for a print cover and haven't read that book just keep in mind that Amazon's template includes bleed, but Ingram's does not. So check that box accordingly.

PREFLIGHT

There are times when File->Export will not bring up the Export Settings dialogue box. Instead you will get an error message that says, "Preflight Warnings: Your document has unresolved preflight errors." This happens all the time with print interiors, but is generally more rare when dealing with advertising images.

When it has happened to me it is usually because one of the images in my ad is below the DPI that I set for the file. It can also be because you scaled an image and didn't keep it proportional.

If you choose to Open Preflight, Affinity will open the Preflight studio which will include any issues in the document. Like here where it is telling me I have one image in my file where the DPI is too low, which means it may be blurry, and that I have one where the scaling was not proportionate which means the image may look "off".

EXPORT, SAVE, AND MORE

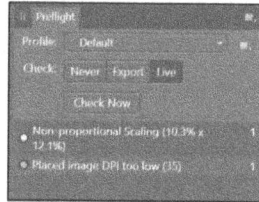

If the final product looks fine to you, because we're working on a computer screen and your end viewer will also be on a screen, you can probably just ignore the preflight issues and continue.

But I created this error and I can see on my screen that the low DPI one would need to be fixed. It's bad enough that I can't tell what the image is supposed to be.

If you double-click on the error in the preflight studio, it should highlight the layer with the problem.

Both of these issues can be fixed using the Transform studio to change the image dimensions.

For the low DPI image you can scale the image until the error message goes away, so reduce H or W with Lock Aspect Ratio turned on until the message disappears.

For the non-proportional scaling, Shift and double-clicking on one of the side borders will return the image to a proportionate size.

Or sometimes I just turn *off* Lock Aspect Ratio and then adjust either H or W until that message disappears.

With either of these errors, you will need to reevaluate your final image to make sure it didn't mess anything up when you fixed that component.

Your other option when that error appears is to simply ignore and continue your export. If things look good to you and it's for an online image, then do so. But take an extra careful look at your final product to be sure.

If it's for print, DO NOT trust what you see on the screen. Print a physical copy for review. Something can look clear on screen but be blurry printed.

SAVE

To save your Affinity file go to File->Save, choose your location and name for your Affinity file, and then click on Save. Ctrl + S also works.

LINKED IMAGES

Be careful if you later move where you have the images you used to create your ad saved. If the files were linked instead of embedded, the next time you open your file, Affinity will tell you that it can't find those images and will give you an opportunity to identify the new location for the images. If you don't provide a new location for the image(s) it will export a blurred image in place of the images it can't find.

This should be pretty obvious for an ad like the ones we've discussed, because everything is right there for you to see. (It's sometimes harder to catch in a print book with lots of images.)

If you notice a blurred image but Affinity didn't ask you to replace it, go into the Resource Manager, find the entry for that image, and use Replace to tell Affinity the new location for the image.

WRAP-UP

Okay, so that's basically how to put together images for ads or websites, etc. in Affinity Publisher. Other than the three-dimensional cover issue, Publisher is more than sufficient to let you put together any advertising image you need.

Just remember what your goal is in creating any sort of ad image. And that's to attract your type of reader and get them to buy or download your book. (Or sign up for your newsletter if that's your goal.) You want your type of person to act.

So with everything you do, ask "will this attract my readers and will they act if it does?" If not, fix it.

And, yes, I'm well aware that's easier said than done. I've been at this a number of years and I'm still not sure I know who my type of reader is for anything I write. So sometimes it's a matter of shooting blind and then judging the results and then adjusting and trying again.

For example, I had a FB ad that did very well at getting readers of George RR Martin to click. But they didn't buy. So they weren't my readers. Or if they were, something on my book page turned them away.

I've also had AMS ads that did very well at getting Sarah J. Maas readers to buy the first book in my fantasy series. But if my also-boughts can be believed, they didn't go on to buy book two so they weren't really my readers. They were fantasy readers, but I didn't give them what they wanted for them to continue reading my books.

So an ad and its visible performance (clicks) is just the beginning. You have to then figure out if that ad really brought in *your* readers.

Okay? Make sense?

The Appendix, as I mentioned before, has quick takes for everything we covered here. So if you want to use one of these skills like, Add a Picture Frame, you don't have to reread that whole section, just check the Appendix.

Also, there is a video version of this course available on Teachable at https://ml-humphrey.teachable.com/courses. Use code MLH50 to get fifty percent off of the cost of the course.

And if you enjoyed this book and want to continue to expand your image design skills using Affinity Publisher then check out *Affinity Publisher for Basic Book Covers* where I will walk you through how to design some basic covers as well as how to take an ebook cover and create print covers for KDP paperback, IngramSpark paperback, and IngramSpark hard cover.

Alrighty then. Good luck with it. Reach out if you get stuck.

APPENDIX A: AFFINITY PUBLISHER QUICK TAKES

BACKGROUND COLOR

ADD

See Rectangle Insert and then Color Apply Specific.

COLOR

APPLY SPECIFIC

To apply a specific color use the Color studio. Double-click on the filled circle or doughnut, whichever is on top, to open the Color Chooser dialogue box. Enter your specific values in the fields for RGB, HSL, CMYK, or the color's hex value next to the # sign. For bright yellow I use FFD500.

CHANGE

For text and fill color there will often be a rounded rectangle in the dynamic menu bar at top showing the current color. Click on that to see a dropdown menu of color choices. The Swatches tab is best for black, white, and shades of gray as well as recent colors used in the document. The Color tab is good for all other solid colors. The eyedropper on the Color tab can be used to choose a color from the canvas. Click on the color swatch you want or into the rectangle of shaded colors in the Color tab to apply. For the eyedropper, double-click on the color next to the eyedropper to apply.

ELEMENTS

CENTER

Layers studio. Select element or elements. Alignment dropdown in top menu. Align Center under Align Horizontally to center left to right or Align Middle under Align Vertically to center top to bottom.

DISTRIBUTE EVENLY

Place left-most and right-most or top-most and bottom-most elements at the outer edge of desired range. Select all elements in the Layers studio.

Alignment dropdown in top menu. Align Horizontally, Space Horizontally to distribute evenly left to right. Align Vertically, Space Vertically to distribute evenly top to bottom.

GROUP AND MOVE

Layers studio. Group layers. Move Tool. Left-click and drag.

GROUP AND RESIZE

Layers studio. Group layers. Click on grouped layers in workspace. Left-click and drag from blue circles around perimeter.

EXPORT

JPG

Go to File and then Export. Choose JPEG at the top of the dialogue box. Set Quality to around 85. Click on Export. Navigate to where you want to export the file. Edit the name if needed. Click on Save.

PNG

Go to File and then Export. Choose PNG at the top of the dialogue box. Click on Export. Navigate to where you want to export the file. Edit the name if needed. Click on Save.

FILE

NEW

Ctrl + N or go to File and then New in the top menu. Or you can choose New Document when you open Affinity.

OPEN

Ctrl + O or go to File and then Open. Navigate to the file, click on it, click on Open. For a file that was recently open you can go to File and then Open Recent and choose the file from the secondary dropdown menu.

SAVE

Ctrl + S or go to File and then Save in the top menu. To rename or save the file to a new location go to File and then Save As.

GUIDE LINES

ADD

Left-click and drag from the ruler around the workspace onto the canvas. Dragging from the top will add a horizontal line. Dragging from the left side will add a vertical line.

REMOVE

Left-click and drag the guideline off of the workspace. If you can't select the guideline, make sure that the Move Tool is selected first.

IMAGE

CONVERT TO BLACK AND WHITE

Select image layer in Layers studio. Go to Layer then New Adjustment and Black & White. Or click on the Layer Adjustments half-filled circle at the bottom of the Layers studio and choose Black & White from the dropdown menu there.

FLIP

Select the image layer. Go to Layer, then Transform, and then choose Flip Horizontal or Flip Vertical.

INSERT

Place Image Tool. Select image to insert. Open. Image may automatically insert. If not, click and drag in workspace until desired size.

INSERT IN PICTURE FRAME

Click on picture frame layer. Place Image Tool. Select image to insert. Open. Image will insert in frame.

LOCK ASPECT RATIO

In the Transform studio left-click on the two links with a small bar connecting them to the right side of the fields for the W and H values. If Lock Aspect Ratio is enabled there will be a line that extends from the links and connect them to the two fields. If it is not enabled there will just be the two links.

MOVE

Move Tool. Click in center of four arrows in center of image or on image layer or directly on image if not in a picture frame. Hold left-click and drag to desired location. Use snapping to align along edges or center. You can also use the Transform studio to move to a specific X or Y location.

REPLACE

Document top menu option. Resource Manager. Select image. Replace. Select new image. Open. Close resource manager.

RESIZE

Move Tool. Click on image layer or directly on image if not in a picture frame. Option A: Transform studio. Lock Aspect Ratio. Change height or width value. Option B: Click on blue circle in corner and drag at an angle to resize proportionately. Or click on blue circle along any edge to change height or width only. This will skew most images.

RESIZE IN PICTURE FRAME

If you are clicked into the picture frame layer there will be a slider below the frame. You can move the slider to the right or left to resize the image in the picture frame.

ROTATE

Select the image layer. Go to Layer, Transform, Rotate Right or Rotate Left. Or go to the Transform studio and enter a value for R. Or left-click on the white filled circle outside the perimeter of the image and hold that left-click as you drag to the right or the left.

SEPIA

Apply Black & White layer adjustment to the image layer. Then go to Layer and Layer Effects or click on the Layer Effects option at the bottom of the Layers studio. Check the box for Color Overlay. Click on the text for Color Overlay. Change Opacity to approximately 50%. Change the color to a darker golden-toned brown color.

LAYER

DELETE

Right-click on the layer in the Layers studio and select Delete from the dropdown menu or click on the layer and use the Delete key.

DUPLICATE

Right-click on the layer in the Layers studio and select Duplicate from the dropdown menu.

GROUP

Select the layers you want to group using the Ctrl key (for layers that are not adjacent) or the Shift key (for layers that are). Left-click on each layer and hold down Shift or Ctrl as you select the rest. Then use Ctrl + G to group the layers or right-click and select Group from the dropdown menu.

HIDE

Uncheck the box next to the layer name in the Layers studio.

MOVE

Left-click and drag a layer up or down to its desired position. The blue shading will show where the layer will go. You can also use the gray and yellow box images in the top menu to move a layer all the way to the top, all the way to the bottom, or up or down one space.

TRANSPARENCY

To change the transparency of a layer, select it in the Layers studio, click on the dropdown for Opacity at the top of the studio, and then adjust the slider to the desired degree of transparency.

UNGROUP

Right-click on the grouped layers in the Layers studio and choose Ungroup from the dropdown menu. Or use Ctrl + Shift + G.

UNHIDE

Check the box next to the layer name in the Layers studio.

NEW DOCUMENT PRESET

ADD

File->Open to start a new document. Make changes in the New Document dialogue box to create a new layout. Click on the + sign next to Custom at the top of the layout settings.

CHOOSE

In the New Document dialogue box click on the preset and then click on Create. Some presets will be under different headings such as Print, Press Ready, etc. and you will need to click on that heading first.

RENAME

Right-click on the thumbnail for the preset. Choose Rename Preset. Type new name. OK.

PICTURE FRAME

BORDER

Select the picture frame layer in the Layers studio. Make sure the Move Tool is selected. To add a border, in the dynamic menu at the top, click on the white line with a red slash through it to the right of Stroke and change the Width value to the desired width. Click on the colored field next to Stroke to change the color of the line. To remove a border, click on the solid line to the right of Stroke in the dynamic menu and then click on the circle with a red slash through the middle next to Style in the dropdown menu.

INSERT

Picture Frame Rectangle Tool. Click and drag to place picture frame on canvas.

MOVE

Select the picture frame layer in the Layers studio. If the Move Tool is selected, left-click anywhere on the frame in the workspace and drag. If the Text Tool is selected, left-click on the perimeter of the frame and drag. Or use the Transform studio to provide a specific X or Y value.

RESIZE

Select the picture frame layer in the Layers studio. Left-click and drag from any of the blue circles around the perimeter of the frame.

RESIZE FRAME AND IMAGE SIMULTANEOUSLY

Select the picture frame layer in the Layers studio. Left-click and drag from the blue circle outside of the perimeter of the frame in the bottom right corner.

RECTANGLE

INSERT

Rectangle Tool. Left-click and drag on the canvas.

SELECT ALL

SELECT ALL

Ctrl + A.

SNAPPING

ENABLE

Go to the horseshoe shaped magnet image in the top center of the top menu. Click on the dropdown arrow. Check the box next to Enable Snapping.

STAR

SHAPE INSERT

Rectangle Tool dropdown. Star Tool. Left-click and drag on the canvas.

TEXT INSERT

Artistic Text Tool. Glyph Browser. Wingdings font. Double-click on star shape.

STUDIO

ANCHOR

Left-click on studio and drag to the left or right-hand side of the workspace until you see a blue outline appear and then release. To move within a series of tabs, simply left-click and drag.

CLOSE

Go to View and then Studio and select the name of the studio you want to close. Or, left-click on the studio, drag it away from the workspace so that it is a standalone dialogue box, and click on the top right corner to close it.

MOVE

Left-click on studio dialogue box or tab and drag to move to desired location.

OPEN

Go to View and then Studio and select the studio you want.

STUDIO PRESET

ADD NEW

Arrange studios as desired. Go to View in top menu. Then Studio Presets. Add Preset. Type name. OK.

APPLY

Option 1: Go to View in top menu and then Studio Presets and select desired preset. Option 2: Ctrl + Shift + [Number] for the desired preset.

DELETE

Go to View in top menu. Then Studio Presets and Manage Studio Presets. Select preset name. Delete. Close.

RENAME

Go to View in top menu. Then Studio Presets and Manage Studio Presets. Select preset name. Rename. Type in new name. OK. Close.

RESET

To reset to the original studio preset go to View and then Studio and Reset Studio.

SAVE CHANGES

Make desired changes to studio preset arrangement. Go to View in top menu. Then Studio Presets. Add Preset. Type in exact same name as before. OK. Agree to overwrite old preset when prompted.

TEXT

ADD

To add text directly onto your canvas, select the Artistic Text Tool, and then click on the canvas and type. You may need to left-click on the canvas and drag to form an A before you can type.

ADD SPECIAL SYMBOLS OR CHARACTERS

Artistic Text Tool. Click into workspace where desired. Go to the Glyph

Browser. Find desired symbol or character. Double-click on symbol or character to insert.

ALIGNMENT (LEFT TO RIGHT)

Artistic Text Tool. Click on the text layer. Go to the menu choices in the dynamic menu above the workspace. There are four images with lines. Align Left, Align Center, Align Right, or use the dropdown menu for Justify Left, Justify Center, Justify Right, Justify All, Align Towards Spine, Align Away From Spine.

ALIGNMENT (TOP TO BOTTOM)

Artistic Text Tool. Click on the text layer. Go to the menu choices in the dynamic menu above the workspace. Use the dropdown menu for Top Align, Center Vertically, Bottom Align, or Justify Vertically.

ALL CAPS OR SMALL CAPS

Artistic Text Tool. Select the text to be formatted. Go to Character studio. Typography section. Click on the two capital Ts (TT) to apply all caps. Click on the capital T with a lowercase T (Tt) to apply small caps.

FONT

Artistic Text Tool. Select text. Dynamic menu at top, left-hand side. Font dropdown. Choose font. Or select text and go to Character studio font dropdown at top.

LINE SPACING (LEADING)

Artistic Text Tool. Select paragraph. Paragraph studio. Spacing section. Change value in Leading dropdown. Default is usually a good place to start. With design work it's often better to just have each line of text as its own layer so you can manually adjust the spacing between elements.

SIZE

Artistic Text Tool. Select text. Dynamic menu at top, left-hand side. Font size dropdown. Choose size or type in size. Or select text and go to Character studio font size dropdown at top.

WEIGHT

Artistic Text Tool. Select text. Dynamic menu at top, left-hand side. Font weight dropdown. (Will usually default to Regular.) Choose from available weights for that font. Or select text and go to Character studio font weight dropdown at top.

TEXT FRAME

ALIGN OR POSITION

Frame Text Tool or Move Tool. Left-click on text frame and hold as you drag. Look for red and green alignment lines to center or align to other elements in workspace. (Turn on Snapping if there are no red or green lines.) Use Alignment dropdown in top menu to align to workspace, not the dynamic menu bar that applies to actual text.

INSERT

Frame Text Tool on left-hand side. Click and drag in workspace.

RESIZE

Click on text frame layer. Left-click and drag on one of the blue circles around the perimeter of the text. Click and drag at an angle from the corner to keep scaling proportionate.

UNDO

Ctrl + Z. Or you can open the History studio and rewind using the slider or by clicking back onto a prior step.

INDEX

ABOUT THE AUTHOR

M.L. Humphrey is a self-published author with both fiction and non-fiction titles published under a variety of pen names. When she gets stuck on her next fiction project she foolishly decides to write books that only ten people are going to buy, although she does usually learn something interesting in the process so it's worth it in the end.

You can reach her at:

mlhumphreywriter@gmail.com

or at

www.mlhumphrey.com

www.ingramcontent.com/pod-product-compliance
Lightning Source LLC
Chambersburg PA
CBHW080624030426
42336CB00018B/3076